THE PROMISE IN PLAN B

THE PROMISE IN PLAN B:

WHAT WE BRING TO THE NEXT CHAPTER IN OUR LIVES

MARY I. FARR *WITH NOAH VAIL*

Published 2015 by Shorehouse Books
Printed in the United States of America

ISBN 0-692-51316-7
EAN-13 978-069251316-3

Editor, Marna Poole
Cover Design by Nancy L Seeger

For Andra and Christian,
who keep me grounded in reality and love

Table of Contents

Introduction

Several years ago I held a retreat at the Gunflint Lodge in Minnesota's Boundary Waters Canoe Area. This remote and enchanting sanctuary in the Superior National Forest struck me as the perfect setting for a group of twelve women to look at their life paths with an eye toward the future and an appetite for fun. We began the day with my single question:

"How many of you are living your Plan A?" Nobody raised her hand.

So it seems that life offers us plenty of opportunities. It also tests us with setbacks, dead ends, hellos and good-byes. Relationships ebb and flow. Jobs begin and end. Responsibilities mount. Fears emerge. Sickness and losses arise. Most of us find ourselves steering our little ships from one safe harbor to another, searching for continuity and meaning, while scrambling to set our sails for the new leg of the journey. Occasionally, however, we get stuck.

It strikes me that living Plan A falls into the category of urban legend. Rarely do we meet someone whose life has followed a blessedly predictable path to success and happiness. Yet we tend to label each stumbling block we encounter along the way as a personal flop. We (or perhaps the culture that surrounds us) often view upsets and do-overs as the result of our ineptitude, a failure to properly manage goals. I'm convinced that this reaction to a disrupted life is frequently inaccurate and nearly always unhelpful. As a gifted clinical pastoral education supervisor once told me when I began training as a hospital chaplain, "Your work will have less to do with your job description and everything to do with the interruptions."

The Promise in Plan B is grounded in the reality that life tends to be a series of interruptions, and we each possess a wealth of resources to initiate, investigate, and recreate the way we travel through our shifting courses. Unlike predictable job skills, these resources emphasize resilience, courage, imagination, humor, curiosity, and more. Yet it's no small irony that many of our most precious strengths get cast aside in a value system that venerates productivity and achievement. In fact, it's these unsung gifts that hold the real power to enhance the quality of our lives and the ease with which we move from one chapter to the next.

Having chosen spiritual care as my vocation nearly three decades ago, I've spent many years working as a hospital chaplain. The work of a chaplain has been described by noted writer and educator Parker J. Palmer as that of an intimate stranger. A chaplain is likely to appear in the midst of a crisis and almost immediately gets drawn into another's most intimate thoughts and stories. These stories, more often than not, end up pitching patients and those who love them in an entirely new direction with an entirely new life plan.

Many of the chapters that follow began with stories of heartfelt plans that ran off the rails. Yet a hospital setting is far from the only place where life gets interrupted. Marriages, aging, empty nests, job promotions, new homes—the list of possibilities is a long one, though not always gloomy. Many of our directional adjustments result in fruitful and affirming experiences. The biggest challenge appears to be our tendency to resist these shifts in direction, rather than letting them reveal their possibilities. True, not every change is a welcome one. Yet even the sharpest turns have a way of self-correcting or adding a new layer of richness to our travels.

Each chapter ends with "Consider This," a compilation of questions and observations related to the chapter's theme. I encourage readers to take the opportunity to discuss the questions, sharing your own insights and experiences with a trusted friend, a loved one, a support group, or a book club.

Additionally, a journaling section appears at the end of the book for those who would rather explore their reflections solo. In either case, I hope the material will resonate with many and encourage a rich stew of responses from all.

Finally, all the wealth, privilege, and therapy money can buy does not guarantee smooth sailing through our life plans. Some people navigate the bumps effortlessly and without drama. Others cave in to despair. Most of us land somewhere between high anxiety and cautious optimism when it comes to changing course. One thing is certain, though: a sense of humor really helps.

A Word about the Character Noah Vail

This is where my equine muse, Noah Vail, enters the picture. Readers familiar with our last book together, *Never Say Neigh*, might recall that Noah has been working his way through a series of entertaining life plans. Not only has he faced his challenges with great pluck, but he's also taught me a thing or two about fun, friendship, and the value of a good gin rummy game. As evidence of his previously untapped inner strengths, Noah has blossomed into a social media pundit and an Erma Bombeck Humor Writer of the Month—make that Blogger of the Month.

People often ask what I find so intriguing about using a horse as a voice in my writing. Anybody who has grown up with cats, dogs, and other pets can probably tell you about their favorite one. Maybe it was the Labrador retriever that smiled a toothy grin and watched Animal Planet, or the cat that flushed the toilet. In my case, I have owned many horses through the years and have learned that a horse's manners and antics offer valuable information about ourselves. Noah Vail has been no exception to that theory. This charming fellow wakes up every day with a smile on his face capable of overriding any amount of grumbling from me. He loves to wear hats. He adores women (and mares). He has been known to pluck an Egg McMuffin out of an unsuspecting diner's hand, and he's simply a joy to know. Noah also demonstrates a kind of horsey wisdom that indicates how much I have yet to learn about laughter and living fully.

I believe it's no accident that Noah Vail's character appeals to a diverse international audience. His social media fans hail from Israel to Australia, and Brazil to the Netherlands. These fans seem to distinguish his writing as a source of benevolence. I can't help thinking that at the heart of their recognition is a human longing for peace and connection with other another, no matter who they are or where they live on this island home we call Earth. While today's immensely successful modes of communication do connect us and flood us with important information, they also can swamp us with violence, unhappiness, and fear. Noah's character offers a voice of hilarity and healing on those days when the news feels too heavy and the ground seems to be buckling beneath our feet.

These days, Noah continues to grow in wit and wisdom. He would also say that he adds a bit of levity to my tendency toward fretting about matters that don't deserve my energy. Between the two of us, we hope to provide readers with a more or less balanced picture of life's most challenging realities, seasoned with a good measure of joyful and inspiring resolve. Noah, after all, is a kind spirit and a wise fellow, ever searching for his own Plan B. It just happens that he has a disarmingly comical way of seeing the world and guiding the rest of us back to center.

Notes from Noah

Life sometimes presents too many choices. Whether I'm shopping for hair products at the Waconia Feed and Hardware Emporium or exploring career prospects in *Horse and Hound*, I've had a few false starts shaping my next career move, especially since my Plan A literally bit the dust.

Back in the day, a talented American Quarter Horse such as I would have eased into a snappy new career involving speed. That's how I landed on an Oklahoma racetrack, as did a half dozen of my jockeys. While these dustups amounted to nothing more than a misunderstanding over technique, it prompted a rift between yours truly and my trainer. Soon enough, a pink slip from the Oklahoma Racing Department arrived. Bingo—I landed up North in flyover country, trying to figure out what an Oklahoma expat does with a bunch of Minnesota Norwegians and a woman of a *certain* age whom I call Madam.

Not that this misadventure turned out to be a bad thing. Frankly, I've learned that life's unscheduled next-stops require little more than a new perspective. Make that a perspective based on *yes*. In my case, the new path also featured a new business partner and alter ego, Mary Farr. I prefer to call her Madam, as you will see in forthcoming "Noah's Notes" I've placed throughout this book. Fortunately, she too favors this *yes* philosophy that I've been campaigning all 'round.

Yes, after all, is good for friendships. *Yes* broadens the options for great adventure. *Yes* opens the door to new gin rummy games and rousing road trips. Finally, *yes* is the very engine that drives me in exhilarating new directions—some planned; others unforeseen. In both cases, I've learned that all will be well if I choose to come along for the ride. So join us for the ultimate road trip to life's next big discovery.

1

The Temptation to Resist Change

Life is a series of natural and spontaneous changes. Don't resist them—that only creates sorrow. Let reality be reality. Let things flow naturally forward in whatever way they like.
—Lao Tzu

I'm convinced that few of us actually *choose* to change much. Instead, we tend to resist moving with the flow until all else fails. Rarely do we resist, like a woman I knew who simply said no to the altered life that stood before her when her husband died. Instead, she retreated to an empty farmhouse on a remote hilltop. At age ninety-four she had no intention of changing anything, including her cloistered lifestyle. Living with other people would have required more adjustments than she was willing to make. She chose isolation.

I met Florence Sedgwick in the hills of western Wisconsin. Over the decades following her husband's death, she had withdrawn from her small farming community. Only an occasional bit of gossip reminded local residents that she ever lived there. Jason Bauer in the Mondovi Co-Op Equity claimed she buried a fortune under her hay shed. A butcher from Bob's IGA insisted that she was once committed to a mental institution. A World War II veteran in the local nursing home insisted that she set fire to a bunkhouse up the valley on the Werlein farm, a fire that killed her supposedly philandering husband. Nevertheless, after years of speculation, nobody really knew much about Florence, or Flossie, as she chose to be called. All this struck me as curious, because the unpainted fortress she called home was only a few miles from town and within riding distance of the place where I kept my horse Dixie. Every time we rode through the hills, I wondered.

No photos or records of her existed in the local library. No letters or church archives held a reliable history of her. The unkempt footpath leading to her front door testified that nobody came to call. She lived a solitary existence, a hermit who aroused only a modest ripple of curiosity. I heard that a few enterprising journalists from the *Eau Claire Leader Telegram* once tried to interview her for a feature story. However, after a strenuous hike up Flossie's driveway, they found themselves looking down the business end of her twelve-gauge shotgun. To the best of everyone's knowledge, they never went back.

The bizarre tales proliferated. Hence, I probably should have questioned my judgment that June morning when I rode Dixie through fields that I loved and up the lane to her house. The early sun slanted through an old apple orchard, the trees like broken sentries guarding the entrance to her property. A first cutting of hay lay in damp windrows beneath the ground fog. Cows and their calves traversed the hillside, rejoining one another after a night spent scattered throughout the pasture. We passed an abandoned cottage where O'Malley's hired man, Mel Jacobson, used to live. The cats had taken charge ever since Mel had a stroke and moved to the Valley Nursing Home. A litter of kittens tumbled off the front stoop into a neglected bed of daylilies, causing Dixie to spook.

The horse saw her first. That's when he really spooked, vaulting up an embankment and nearly depositing me in the blackberry bushes. By anybody's standards, she was an awesome sight, a wizened gnome stooped in the tall grass. She clutched the handle of a double-bladed ax, convincing me that the earlier shotgun incident probably had happened. Her expression wavered between anger and curiosity as she crouched, poised for combat. She wore a dress secured with large safety pins to several layers of long underwear, much like a homeless woman might manage her shreds of clothing. Her leathery skin hung about her neck and from her muscular arms. Her hands were immense. A pink plastic barrette held her hair off her forehead, while a plain wedding band and wire-rimmed spectacles provided the only clues that she ever interacted with civilization.

By now, Dixie was hopelessly unmanageable, and I needed to either dismount or be thrown. Choosing the first option, I slipped out of the saddle, tied up his reins, and watched him gallop off for home as if he had encountered a ghost. Frankly, I wondered the same. So there I stood, about a dozen feet from the old woman. She gripped her ax but didn't make any threatening moves, nor did she run away. A long moment passed before it occurred to me to offer my hand in a greeting. Surprisingly, she stepped forward, shook my extended hand, and launched a few comments about my horse's thundering exit.

"I'm not surprised he's a-feared of me," she announced simply. "Dogs is too. It's because I'm too old. I've lived too long. But my cat, Jefferson, back home ... well, now, that's a different story. He loves me. Never leaves home for longer than a day. He stays to home the way he should." She kept talking, giving me time to calm down.

I eventually learned that Flossie was born on a small farm in the nearby township of Dover. "Three generations of us have growed up right in this here area," she explained. "My mother was born in a log cabin on the hill behind my place. This is home for me. I'd rather take a pounding than go to town. As far as I'm concerned, I'll be here on my forty, three hundred and sixty-five days a year, 'til the day I die."

This strange encounter marked my first of many visits to Flossie's homestead. As a journalist, I found her fascinating. As a recently divorced, financially struggling mother of two children, I experienced a stunning awakening. Eccentric or not, Flossie had something in common with any of us who ever wanted to run away from pain and responsibility. The primary difference in Flossie was that she never mastered the art of moving forward through change. The losses and setbacks that most people experience during a lifetime drove her in a different direction. Through the years, she slowly withdrew, finally choosing to travel alone rather than risk any more losses or disappointments.

Flossie and her husband, "the Old Gent," began farming their plot in the 1930s. "We worked with the neighbors back then," she said, "especially when we were threshing or shredding. I hauled grain shocks out of the field all day long. After the bundles dried, I'd run the steam thresher to separate the grain from the straw. I've never driven a car, but I can drive any horse or steam engine you could find me."

Flossie chose her own road and then stuck to it ... alone. As she groped through her memories of cooking and harvesting, I could see how each bit of past misfortune had nudged her further from the company of others. During our subsequent visits, she stitched a patchwork account of her history; the Great Depression; crop losses and the Old Gent's death; her children leaving home; automated methods of farming; and a legal battle to keep her beloved forty. Faced with seemingly endless difficult decisions, she focused on the only thing she felt she had left—her homestead.

"I made up my mind long ago I would rally here or perish," she said. "It's quiet here, and it's mine."

There she spent most of her hours, collecting fruits and nuts, chopping brush and splitting firewood for her old Heaterolla stove. Every summer, a local mill delivered ten loads of wood. By fall, she had cut and neatly stacked each piece behind her back porch. Now and then, someone dropped off food and other staples at her mailbox. She loaded the supplies onto a wheelbarrow and pushed it up the half-mile hill. Jars of canned meats and fruits filled her pantry shelf, and large bowls of hand-pumped water lined the countertop. Rags curtained the windows, and braided rugs were scattered on the unfinished wood floor. In a wooden crate next to the pump house slept her loyal companion, Jefferson.

Flossie's story was both troubling and seductive. I saw something deliciously alluring about the idea of vanishing, of casting off the complicated relationships, damage, and responsibilities that sapped me of energy. That trip back to the drawing board to plot a new course for my children and myself had often felt daunting. Yet as she told her story, it was evident that Flossie bore the burden of estrangement and sadness that accompany a choice to retreat. Though she spoke with enthusiasm about her life on the forty, she clearly longed for human contact. And so it happened that Flossie Sedgwick and I became unexpected friends.

Most of the locals were satisfied to call Flossie crazy, but her desire to escape from a broken life was far from unique. The fact is, there's nothing unusual about setting goals and creating plans that bring security and stability to our lives. The trouble arrives when something goes haywire and we get knocked off the rails. That's when we need to stop beating the stuffing out of ourselves over what went wrong, and start mapping a course for the next adventure.

Success, as I've grown to understand it, cannot be measured by what one is or does but only by distance traveled. We are forever moving from one experience to another; one challenge to another; one relationship, loss, or achievement to another. We are unfinished business, reshaped by our continuing experience. It's this fluid quality of life that invites us to become resilient rather than resistant, to belong rather than to retreat. Openness, a receptive heart, and a willingness to let it go help clear the way to something new.

To be open is to make oneself available to life. Openness allows us to drop our past rebuffs and rejections, both our victories and our failures. It helps us to see things afresh, as always newborn and stocked with possibilities. The goal, as I understand it, is to become so open to life that nothing can diminish the joy of discovery.

That ability to handle change and stay connected is a learned asset—a gift that Flossie never embraced. It often demands alterations of the original plan. These changes pull us out of our secure niches and place us in unfamiliar territory. We instinctively want security, even if that security is an unpleasant repetition of past mistakes. The learning comes in letting go of some of the controls we try to apply. The rewards come with discovering those things that we might have missed through our refusal to consider a new way.

There are no written guarantees that things will work out comfortably for us, yet joy comes in an ability to transform and grow together with others in spite of ambiguity. We gain nothing by pulling down the blinds or by giving way to cynicism and despair. How sad it would be for us to go to the kitchen one morning and find there was no bread.

How much more sad it would be if we were to go to the kitchen and find that we weren't hungry.

As I thought about Flossie's life story, I realized how essential it is to belong. Belonging quite literally fosters the courage to keep walking, even when the light ahead seems dim.

At some level, everyone wants to belong, even a recluse such as Flossie. In fact, she eventually had to move to a safer living environment, where she made many meaningful connections with her caretakers and other residents. She, as do each of us, *needs* to belong. We belong to families of countless shapes and sizes. We belong to work groups, support groups, religious organizations, and card clubs. Most certainly we all know what it feels like to belong. Or do we?

Many years have passed since I formally took up a vocation of listening to people talk about their lives—their dreams, their losses, and their unmet needs. For a hospital chaplain, attending to the human story means everything. The stories speak of sickness and health. They describe joy and gratitude as well as success and failure. They touch every possibility—and a few impossibilities—that folks carry with them. These stories infuse every social, economic, and cultural experience one can imagine. Yet while the stories differ widely in their circumstances, they often share a theme: the problem of belonging—or perhaps more accurately, of not belonging.

Hospitals, to me, always have felt like small worlds of their own, mimicking the larger community outside. Hospital populations consist of a mix of health care workers whose lives merge with the lives of patients and families representing every age and culture. Hospitals contain the full measure of life's drama under one roof, from birth to death, sickness to health, and all manner of socioeconomic dilemmas. Day in and day out, the entire range of human needs and behaviors flow through the hallways and nursing units, enacted by everyone from housekeepers to surgeons. Many of the stories shared within this microcosm community speak of a longing to belong.

Our world of instant, incessant and, increasingly, faceless communication also contributes to the larger story of belonging. On one hand, social media and myriad forms of connecting with one another make it easier to belong. On the other hand, advancing technology reflects a sense of disconnection and loneliness. If my observations are accurate, Americans suffer from an eroded sense of belonging. And belonging, I've learned, is essential for good health and the capacity to function fully.

A culture of shifting landscapes and diminishing guideposts has translated to a climate of chronic insecurity. We feel ambivalent about our work. We try to adjust to our persistent anxiousness. We find ourselves looking deeply into our own stories for signs and direction. Where are we? Do we have the capacity to feel "a part of"? Do we possess the resources to connect deeply with one another, or must we go looking for them.

The answer, I believe, is yes, we do have the resources. No, we do not have to look beyond ourselves. However, to tap the wellspring of intimacy for which we hope requires nurturing and maybe even a change of heart. There are simply no quick fixes and no easy answers to fill this need of belonging. Ultimately, there is no path but the path made by our own walking. Part of the way to our belonging lies in our capacity to rediscover our humanity and our inherent human skill to be our brothers' and sisters' keeper. Through this, we learn about our extraordinary ability to create a sense of place for ourselves. We begin to see everyday experiences and relationships in new ways, as rich sources of vitality and sustenance.

Belonging takes work. It sometimes means refashioning our communities on the job and at home, or at least rediscovering the value of wasting time wisely with those we care about. It means including those who are alone. To belong is to move in the direction of the larger whole, not simply toward our own goals and objectives. Belonging invites well-being or, to put it another way, being well.

Consider This: Think About the Power of Belonging

A sense of belonging comes in many shapes and descriptions. Some of us are quick to partake in groups and communities. Others feel comfortable observing from the edges. In either case, the following ideas grew from my conversations with individuals and families searching for ways to belong. While these provide various ideas for moving through transitions, readers no doubt have many more to add when it comes to connecting or reconnecting with others:

- Identify your sources of community.
- Consider new ones.
- Let go of harsh judgments of yourself and others.
- Permit grief when an upset or setback occurs.
- Make space for your story, and share it with another.
- Listen fully to someone who feels unable to make a change.
- Identify small ways to create order in your life.
- Reach out to someone who feels isolated or alone.
- Encourage and advocate for one another.

2

Noah's Notes:

Practice Saying Yes

My poker club, composed of a half dozen antique geldings, was enjoying an evening of five-card draw with a side of morning-glory pizza recently when Madam showed up at the party-room door. She usually avoided my card club nights, and I understood why. After a long winter swaddled in a Rambo stable blanket, a couple of our malodorous players needed a proper bath. So imagine my surprise when she pulled up a chair and settled in. It was Gabe's turn to deal.

"So I've been wondering about something," said Madam as she helped herself to a slice of pizza. "How many of you guys are working on your Plan A?"

Oh dear, here we go again, I thought.

Everyone paused mid-chew. Gabe laid down the cards and glanced around the table for a sign that anyone knew what she was talking about. Arrow eyed me with a bewildered expression. Omar gawked at Spruce. Gilbert, whose head barely cleared the table, fixed a befuddled gaze on Madam. She made a quick assessment of the baffled looks and started over.

"What I'd like you to do is raise your hoof if you started out life with a particular career or personal plan in mind and, if so, are you still chasing that same plan?"

Just as in her previous experience with the women's retreat, nobody raised a hoof. Since she and I had already covered this topic ad nauseam, I could see that she was now angling for a focus group composed of my poker club—an unusual source of research, I might add.

So the boys pondered her question in silence. Finally, I felt compelled to end the awkward moment by shouting out an example for the others. "Well, one could say that I started out with a Plan A to win a million dollars on the racetrack," I offered. "As you can see, this is no Hialeah Park."

"Yup, that plan and your jockey bit the dirt at just about the second mile post," declared Spruce, with a louder-than-necessary guffaw. "And if memory serves, you're now employed as a life coach for an adolescent Jack Russell terrier. That's quite a leap between plans, if you ask me."

True.

"How about you, Gabe?" queried Madam.

"Hmm ... well, I once enjoyed a brush with stardom, riding to the hounds in Virginia," he recalled wistfully. "Then someone got the bright idea that I'd be great at law enforcement. That ended after a Minnesota Vikings and Green Bay Packers game when I got fired for sipping a brewski while working crowd control. Now I play a lot of cards and bet on all those horses that Noah left in the dust."

"And the rest of you?" asked Madam hopefully.

"Well, I once could jump over the moon," exclaimed Spruce to nobody in particular. "That was until I blew out my knee chasing a possum out of the pasture. Now I hang out at Minnetonka Orchard, giving hayride tours and playing a little touch Hoofleball."

On it went, until everyone at the table had described an adventure or misadventure that pointed them to Plan B, C, or Z that eventually landed them at Fortuna Farm.

So I couldn't help wondering how things might have turned out, had each of us not fallen off the rails and into the abyss of change. I guess we'll never know, but one thing's for sure: it was good that I said yes to the plan that followed my exit from racing. Otherwise, I'd not be spending Monday nights playing five-card draw with a grand bunch of mates and a woman who wears spurs to the grocery store and taught me how to make morning glory pizza.

3

Make Time for Community

Without a sense of caring, there can be no sense of community.
—Anthony J. D'Angelo

A physiologist whose research focused on the human heart once offered me a provocative piece of information: "When you place cells from two separate hearts into a single incubating medium, they begin to communicate with one another."

It seems that certain proteins in heart-cell membranes enable the cells to communicate with one another. Unlike other body cells, those that make up the human heart can transfer electrical energy from cell to cell. Once placed in a petri dish, the faster-beating cells tell the slower-beating cells to speed up until, eventually, the two kinds beat in unison, as one. Compelling evidence that at the very center of our beings, we humans are quite literally connected. So after all the science and technology has been applied, and all the quality assurance metrics benchmarks have been met, our mission in life comes down to just one thing—we simply cannot fail when we choose to connect with and care for one another. And caring for one another requires building and maintaining meaningful bonds through community. This lesson came early in my professional life, about the time I was unceremoniously dismissed from what I once thought was an important job.

Nothing delivers a load of crushed confidence quite like getting fired. From where I stood, the boss, who assured me that our company's downsizing was "nothing personal," had no idea what he was talking about. It felt *very* personal on my end and stirred emotions ranging from shock to withering humiliation. And that was before I undertook the difficult job search and rejections that followed.

So what if it was a budget decision that led to my exit? An unplanned separation from a work environment, even a difficult one, creates consequences far beyond a lost paycheck. In this case, it separated me from a community of colleagues with whom I'd connected on a daily basis. Whether we share responsibilities, work in teams, or join our peers for happy hour, these daily links to others really do matter, and losing a job divorces us from much more than revenue. For better or worse, it disrupts our community.

To say that community fosters well-being is to say that July brings mosquitoes to Minnesota. Community provides an essential ingredient for maintaining balance and happiness. All the remote methods of communicating we find at our fingertips cannot replace face-to-face interaction with communities that matter.

While I might not have appreciated that abrupt dismissal from a well-paying corporate job, I've always appreciated the rare little community of hospital chaplains with whom I worked for many years. This group realized early in our relationship that if we valued the benefits of community, we had better make a genuine attempt to live it. Our goal turned out to be good news but not always easy news.

The team of five looked like an affirmative-action poster. We were a curious stew of cultures, colors, ages, and spiritual traditions. And if those contrasts weren't challenging enough, add a broad range of communication styles. Over-committed and often overworked, most of us had other professional responsibilities outside the children's hospital in which we worked. We were singularly opinionated, dedicated, sometimes silly, and often irreverent. Fortunately, we all appreciated our work and one another. Yet our differences meant we had to listen more carefully, negotiate more fully, and build plans more thoughtfully. Imagine such a model operating within our country's political or education system. True, it required more work, but we all appreciated the rewards.

So with an eye on harmony and a determination to succeed together, we worked hard at maintaining community, both inside the hospital and among ourselves. We talked often, sharing personal and professional wins and losses. We hung out together as much as was reasonable. At least once a month, we spent the evening together away from the hospital. We didn't use this time to discuss quality improvements or census numbers. These get-togethers were designed for serious fun as well as heartfelt conversations. Sometimes our families came, and sometimes we came alone. It mattered little who or how many appeared at the table. Occasionally, curious newcomers joined us and had such a good time they came back permanently. Showing up was the only requirement. When I purchased a new home, the group wrote blessings for every spot and corner, from the kitchen stove to the bathtub and even our family dog. Other times, we toasted the birth of a first child or cheered on a pending marriage. Our evenings proved to be a potent prescription for the isolation and exhaustion that sometimes left us ragged at the end of a long day.

In truth, the place in which we met spoke of hospitality, which brightened our professional community. Hospitality enjoys a long relationship with the concept of a hospital. Established by early monastic communities and often connected with churches, hospitals served as havens for weary travelers, welcoming oases offering food and rest to anyone who needed either.

Hospitality, then, anticipates the arrival of guests; it is not a ten-word text on a smartphone. It requires a welcoming heart that knows and accepts our own and another's incompleteness. To offer hospitality within community is to weave together a common cloth of gladness as well as defeat. Hospitality invites us to keep dreaming.

Consider This: Why Community Matters

We live in a time when considerable value has been attached to rugged individualism. Don't cry. Don't risk revealing your authentic self. Win often. Crave much. Do well. Attain more. Wear the brave mask or whatever mask disguises your essential self. This kind of individualism can crush the heart of community by dismissing it as irrelevant and time-consuming.

Community exists within any intimate group. A community can be little or big, biologically or spiritually related, or professionally connected. Community furnishes the mortar that binds up human brokenness. It restores our hope and fuels our desire to keep on keeping on. A community consists of those who choose to be together so that they might communicate deeply and honestly with one another. Community meets people where they are—rejoicing, sharing frustrations, or mourning losses. It asserts that individuality and interdependence are not mutually exclusive. In short, it calls us to become fully ourselves while remaining joined to another or others. Community nourishes children while it sustains adults and protects fragile elders.

Impractical as it sometimes seems, when it's so easy to Skype someone on our iPads, we really benefit from getting together. Refreshment lies in celebrating the fundamentals with others and restoring parts of our selves depleted by daily responsibilities. It might seem a small and unnecessary thing, but it helps—even if it's nothing more than a book club that has stopped reading the books but still enjoys sharing a nice glass of Chianti Classico and a plate of marinated mozzarella.

Historically, we don't much like diversity. One look at the daily news or listening to the political rhetoric tells us we tend to like sameness. Yet what is it that we like about sameness? What can be gained by opening our minds and hearts to diversity? Why do we find it so hard to negotiate conflicting viewpoints within our various cultural and other communities?

Which of the following do you feel create the most gridlock within our communities and institutions, and how might these be reframed into a more constructive approach to working together?

- We are in a rush for immediate solutions, and negotiating takes time.
- Most people prefer to skip compromise in favor of achieving their own goals.
- Some ideas are so bad, they don't deserve consideration.
- Negotiating tends to water down great ideas.
- Most people prefer to avoid conflict.
- Apathy often colors conflict resolution.

4

Bruce and Sue Kerfoot—A Time for Tenacity

An infinitesimal speck in the cosmos, I stood on the shore of Gunflint Lake beneath a great white pine—matriarch of a fast vanishing tribe. And I knew I was home. I was twenty-one. The year was 1927.

—Justine Kerfoot

So wrote Justine Kerfoot in her memoir of sixty years along the Gunflint Trail, nestled in the Boundary Waters Canoe Area. Once a city girl with aspirations of becoming a physician, Kerfoot instead became one of the last pioneers of the North Woods. Today, her son, Bruce, embodies his mother's dream with a singular level of love for the land, commitment to service, and tenacity in challenging times.

"She was a pioneer as unique as they come," said Bruce, who, with his wife, Sue, now runs a thriving Gunflint Lodge that began as a small 1920s fishing camp with no electricity or indoor plumbing. "She was a pioneer in the sense we don't even know in our generation—for the frontier she lived in and the challenges that faced all of the few residents. And she took them on as a woman, which was more unusual than anything else."

Born in a rustic log cabin and a world of dogsleds, fishing expeditions, and grinding work, Bruce described their way of life in the remote wilderness. The property included three log cabins for rent, a dining room, an owner's cabin, and a staff cabin. A small lodge with a store stocked supplies for their Native American neighbors and fishing tackle for the guests. For years, the forty-three-mile road to Grand Marais, Minnesota, never saw a snow plow. Bruce and his two sisters were homeschooled, and he remembers his mother helping him with homework as she repaired a piece of machinery or fixed the plumbing.

"We learned to live on our own merits," said Bruce. "We entertained ourselves. We solved our own problems. It was a very independent way of life."

Only for the last years of high school did Bruce attend public school in Grand Marais. And once he graduated, he encountered the first pivotal point in his young life that landed him in a new plan. He applied and was accepted at Cornell University's prestigious School of Hotel Administration.

"I didn't have a clue what kind of challenge I was jumping into at Cornell," said Bruce. "I was about to take my first plane ride from hayseed to Ivy League. My dad drove me to Duluth and saw me off. It was when he handed me a brand-new Dopp kit that I realized I had nothing to put in it. We didn't even have indoor plumbing."

That transition from backwoods to the firing line of one of the finer schools in the East came as quite a shock. While his roommate's parents delivered a new wardrobe to their son twice a year, Bruce slipped by with a country boy's basics and two modest sport coats. Then came an even bigger shock when he failed his first exam in a high-credit course. Things looked even less encouraging the next day, when Cornell's president announced to Bruce's freshman class that only 33 percent of them would graduate.

"At that moment, I truly wondered what I had got myself into," Bruce admitted. "Yet in my family, we didn't know the word quit. We only focused on solutions."

Challenging or not, he survived academically, learned from his classmates, and charmed them with stories about his unusual life among moose and grey wolves. Four years later, he had gained a remarkable education that would serve him well. Yet rather than pursue an urbane career in the hospitality industry, he fulfilled his two-year military commitment and returned home to the Gunflint. Equipped with a new set of tools and a desire to create, Bruce went to work transforming his family's austere fishing camp into a haven of beauty and hospitality. He and his family worked hard to get through that winter. They were like farmers with one point of income. Beyond that, they were broke. He and his mother, Justine, took on the tasks of pounding nails and figuring out how to make the place grow.

Unfortunately, Bruce's wife felt less passionate about the hard labor and remote living. It soon became clear this was not a life she cared to live. Eventually, she packed up and departed for Saint Paul, leaving Bruce and their two children behind. It devastated the entire family and added a whole new challenge to building their home and future.

"I felt pretty low," Bruce admitted, "as low as I've ever felt."

But then, his wife wrote and invited him to come with the children to Saint Paul, with the prospect of reconciliation. He immediately agreed and rushed to the city in hope of finding a second chance to preserve his marriage. The first day or two seemed to go well—or so he thought. Yet by day three, Bruce faced a painful truth: there would be no reconciliation. His wife sent him on an errand, and while he was out, she gathered up the children and left. Bruce headed back home alone, at a complete loss.

Time passed, and he worked hard. "You heal," he recalled. "You put the pieces back together and start making a new plan. I marched ahead, building and 'batching it' for a couple of years."

That's when he met Sue—"number two," as Bruce put it. Lured to the North Star state by Saint Olaf College, Sue had spent two summers working at the Gunflint Lodge gift shop. Not until much later, after she graduated and returned to work in Chicago, did she and Bruce discover one another and their future together. They married in 1968, and Sue has partnered with Bruce as wife, friend, trusted business collaborator, and fellow adventurer traveler ever since.

The two marched along, working side by side. "It was a big change for me," Sue admitted. "No weekends, no weekend planning. I loved the lodge, but I had quarrels with it when I was younger. You are always on call. There is no such thing as taking a day off. I wasn't always the gracious adjustee," she added with a wry smile.

Their work paid off, and the business kept growing. Bruce and Sue welcomed their firstborn son, David. Hard work and a new baby brought a new level of joy to the couple in those first months.

"Then one day in September, I walked back to look at David in his crib and realized he was not breathing," said Bruce. "He had died. Our first baby died of sudden infant death syndrome."

"It happened out of the clear blue," Sue continued. "Nowadays mothers are taught how to place their babies in the crib, but this was not the case in the '60s. The loss had many lasting effects on me, including the fact that while the child was dying, I was washing pots and pans in the lodge. It took me a long time before I could wash pots and pans in the lodge again."

"It tore at our life but not at our marriage," Bruce asserted.

"There was no way to change it," said Sue. "I could do nothing except move on. So I did. We did."

Shortly after David's death, Bruce and Sue accepted an invitation to join a friend who led tours in Europe. They took the time to be alone, where there was no pressure to explain anything, including what had happened. It proved to be a first step toward healing for both of them.

"It gave us a chance to relax, sleep, and do nothing," said Sue. "We were fortunate to have good friends who supported us through this loss. We not only survived it, [but] our marriage survived, and we welcomed a second child, Robert, in

September the following year. Bruce and I were both ready for it and willing to move on with our lives." A third arrived just a year later.

Through the years, their rustic little fishing camp has flourished. It's grown into an enchanting year-round resort that Bruce fondly refers to as a perpetual construction project. He has rebuilt every cabin at least once. The main lodge was winterized in the early 1990s, when they began hosting winter cross-country skiers. Classic cabins, luxurious lakeside cabins, and bunkhouses serve as temporary homes to BWCA guests and die-hard canoeists. The Towering Pines Canopy Tour offers eight zip lines that thread between pine-scented tree platforms, fifty feet above ancient rock formations, shimmering streams, white-tail deer, and an occasional moose cow with her calf. The business keeps growing.

Bruce and Sue have always been passionate about sharing nature with their guests and implemented a naturalist program more than forty years ago. They also participate in a J1 seasonal hiring program involving students from many countries who come on short-term visas to experience American life and bring cultural diversity to American businesses. The Gunflint has hosted employees from Turkey, Croatia, France, Bali, Jamaica, and beyond.

Eventually, Bruce and Sue felt confident enough to flirt with the idea of retirement. This meant handing over Gunflint operations to their two sons. Both appeared ready and willing to come home and go to work—with one possible exception: neither of their wives found the North Woods as enchanting as did the rest of the family. In short, it didn't work.

"We forgot the formula," said Bruce. This kind of life and work together anticipates a commitment from everyone to both the hospitality business *and* to wilderness living. Northern lights and natural beauty aside, calling the Gunflint Trail home does not suit everyone. Not only did Bruce and Sue have to retrieve the organization's reins, but they also had to rebuild the business lost during their sons' youthful foray into resort management. And so, retirement would have to wait.

"Actually, our friends claimed we flunked retirement," chuckled Sue. "We didn't have a backup plan." Little did she know that their interrupted retirement wasn't the only hurdle that lay ahead. "Bruce said to me, don't worry; we will make it right. And we did."

"We had to put the company back together," said Bruce. And so he and Sue mapped out a new plan to save it.

"We never discussed whether we could make it," said Bruce. "We just talked about how we were going to do it. Success is like climbing a mountain. You either keep looking up and moving ahead, or you're likely to fall."

They have indeed kept looking up and moving ahead. They've doubled the Gunflint Lodge's growth, even during the economic downturn. They continue to explore new ideas, even during Sue's bout with breast cancer. They greet diners in the lodge dining room every night, even though Bruce flunked a cardiac stress test resulting in a heart bypass, accompanied by an aortic aneurism. What's more, they have never lost their gusto for adventure travel. The two have climbed the Himalayas, taken three African safaris, hiked in Bhutan, visited Turkey three times, and rented homes in Bali and the island of Majorca for months at a time.

"I've seen many examples of people waiting until late in life to have some fun," said Bruce. "Then something happens, and they can't."

Through tenacity and creative problem solving, Bruce and Sue Kerfoot have built and preserved their Plan A dream. According to Sue, the term *innovative* typically comes up when people speak of Bruce.

"When you work for Bruce Kerfoot, there's always change. He can come up with a hundred different ideas, and he doesn't care if ninety-nine of them fail, as long as one succeeds."

Both remain active within the broader Boundary Waters Canoe Area, helping friends and neighbors and mentoring other lodge owners. Their work has garnered them abundant awards and accolades. Bruce has been a delegate to the White House Conference on Tourism, received a presidential appointment to the National Recreational Trail Advisory Board, and presented testimony to a US House of Representatives subcommittee. Sue writes a wilderness blog highlighting seasons, wildlife sightings, fishing reports, and tourism activities. She also cowrote *The Gunflint Lodge Cookbook* and serves as historian for the Gunflint Trail Historical Society. She was instrumental in the creation and operation of the Chik-Wauk Museum and Nature Center, which highlights the natural and cultural history of the Gunflint Trail. The two have been inducted into the Minnesota Hospitality Hall of Fame for their lifetime achievement and exemplary leadership. Today, their list of interests and achievements keeps growing.

Justine Kerfoot came from a wealthy Chicago family, a life overflowing with classic automobiles, charming homes, and debutante balls. The stock market crash of 1929 ruined them financially, leaving Justine with no money and a worn-out fishing lodge tucked into the US shoreline of Gunflint Lake. There, she learned to hunt moose, drive dogsleds, and re-canvas canoes, while befriending Native American neighbors. More than eighty years later, Justine's son and daughter-in-law continue to represent the integrity and character of this country—strong, independent, and grateful to have to have spent their lives in a place they love with a Plan A they have finally mastered.

Consider This: Explore the Road You're On

It's so easy to drift through life paying scant attention to our situations and surroundings. One day, we're twenty-five years old, charging out to join the flow. The next, so it seems, we realize that time has moved forward, though we have not. Even when life feels comfortable and secure, it's helpful to take stock of where we've been and where we hope to go. Have we been tenacious, following our dreams? Or have we remained stubbornly stuck to the old and familiar methods of interacting with life?

- What are some of the dreams you had in your twenties? Forties? Sixties?
- Have you realized some of these dreams? Which ones?
- What has it been like for you to be unable to fulfill some of your dreams?
- What are your dreams and hopes at the moment?
- Are there people and/or expectations that make it difficult for you to let go and move on?
- If you had only one year left to live, how would you spend the time?
- Are there relationships in your life that need healing?
- What aspects of the relationship make it hard to forgive yourself or another?

5

A Reason to Hope

Learn from yesterday, live for today, hope for tomorrow.
The important thing is not to stop questioning.
—Albert Einstein

A Scottish woman once sent me the following poem, a perfect little jewel that I have returned to examine oh-so-many times.

> I said to the night
> that stood at the gate of the new year,
> "Give me a light
> that I might tread safely
> into the dark and unknown."
> And a voice said in reply,
> "Put your hand into the hand of the one who made you,
> and your reward will be
> blessed with more light
> far safer
> than the unknown."

When I asked her the meaning of hope, this wise woman told me, "Most people associate hope with optimism. I find it more helpful to define the optimist as someone who says everything is going to be fine. The pessimist says everything will be awful. The hopeful person says, 'However things shall be, it will bring forth life.'"

This must be true, for there are many situations in which we have no reason for optimism but every reason for hope.

One of those occasions took place in the month of January. The young parents in the emergency room where I worked watched without words as a team of physicians, pharmacists, respiratory therapists, nurses, and more labored over their baby boy. Hoping against hope, the family members gripped each other's hands and prayed for a miracle that would revive their son.

Born just a few weeks earlier, baby Jorden had been diagnosed with hemophilia, though by all accounts he was doing very well. Surprised at their good fortune of a later-in-life pregnancy, both Jorden's parents and his older siblings were thrilled at the baby boy's arrival. The instant he emerged from his mother's womb, Jorden became the center of his family's adoration. His ecstatic parents clucked attentively over his every move, keeping a watchful eye on all aspects of his care. What good fortune that their new life chapter included a son.

On this morning, however, something had gone terribly wrong. Somewhere between a family's rejoicing at breakfast over their baby and their drive home from visiting with relatives, Jorden died. He produced not a sound, not a seizure, not a hint of warning. He simply stopped breathing. More shocking, his father did not discover the catastrophe until he parked the car in the garage and reached into the backseat to lift Jorden from his infant seat. In an instant, the mystery of love that created him and prepared a place for him was about to come to terms with letting him go.

After rushing Jorden to the hospital, and after what seemed like an interminable hour, the emergency room physician in charge of resuscitation efforts stopped and looked helplessly into the parents' faces. It was hardly necessary for her to speak, as everyone had known—or at least had suspected—the outcome before the painstaking attempt to revive Jorden even began. The rest of the trauma team backed away from the baby, paralyzed by disbelief. It was sudden infant death syndrome. It was over.

What happened next, however, would transform this shattering loss into an experience of a very different nature. Jorden's parents turned to the large assembly of health care professionals and thanked each person in the room for her or his valiant effort to save Jorden's life. The couple then thanked each other for the life they had shared for many years. They thanked their family physician and the clinic nurses who had provided Jorden's ongoing care. They even thanked the paramedics who raced to their home and toiled in vain to breathe life back into Jorden.

Finally, though tearful and shaky, Jorden's father gently wrapped his son in a clean receiving blanket, lifted the baby upward toward the blinding trauma-room lights, and thanked God for sharing Jorden with him and his family. He then baptized the lifeless child. It was a gesture of gratitude that brought the normally bustling emergency department to a standstill. The tables had turned. A family who had lost more than words could say had extended a healing hand and heartfelt expression gratitude to the professional caregivers.

"There is no tragedy, nor is there any kind of loss, through which life cannot come forward," said Jorden's father several weeks later. "Sometimes we simply have no control, and all we can do is try to go on living our lives with integrity. Jorden's death was outside of our control, but we trust that life can come from it. We know grace can somehow come from it." And it did.

Several months later, Jorden's physician was to offer the address at a hospital memorial service held for all the families whose children had died in the past year. Before an auditorium full of pensive parents and grandparents, he spoke about mercy and gratitude and how important a role both of these played in the practice of medicine. He then thanked the families for teaching him about children and for allowing him to care for their children. He described how much it meant to him that they shared their wisdom about loss with him. Then he told a story about the death of his father.

What a long and difficult path the two had walked together through his father's treatment for debilitating heart disease. The doctor described how the two of them had made a point of expressing their appreciation for the blessings of their shared life. He spoke honestly about how it felt to have no cure to offer. Eventually, he told the story of his father's last hours, the bathing and gently turning him and changing of his bedclothes. He massaged his father's feet and hands, offering all the tender care that prevails when clinical practice becomes moot. At the end, each man said thank you to the other and to the silence. And then they said good-bye.

After witnessing both of those events, I realized that there are some things in life we can take into our hands and hold up to the light or put under a microscope for a clearer understanding. We can sift through a handful of shells or inspect a beautiful piece of silk. We can imagine the magnificence of a masterful painting; we can observe the petals of a rose. But there are other matters that we cannot grasp with our hands or eyes but only with our hearts. These extend beyond our reach and our comprehension. They carry us past the conscious world of familiar scenery and sounds into the silent world of the unknown. Some would describe these experiences as encounters with mystery, the revelation of something hidden. In the case of Jorden's family and the physician, the mystery originated in their posture of openness to all of life, even life blessed and broken. Father to son. Son to father. Theirs was an unbroken circle, a connection of the heart that began in life and remained in death.

Jorden died in the month of January. January receives its name from Janus, the god of thresholds. Janus is often pictured with two faces. One face looks backward in memory, and the other face searches the horizon of the future. Janus is also the patron of doorways. The month that bears his name marks the season of endings and beginnings, as in the beginning of a new year. It is the time of inventories. January is the month of resuming old routines after the holidays and starting new ones that sustain us through the rest of the winter and, perhaps, onto a new road.

Crossing the January threshold and beginning anew must have been painful for Jorden's family. Beginnings and endings never come easily. Adjusting life plans and reshaping lost dreams takes tremendous courage. Accepting an unwelcome reality stood before Jorden's family. These are the trials that make us wonder if we should stretch out our hands and welcome another day, or just turn over and pull the blanket over our heads. Shall we hide from life, or shall we embrace it?

Most of us experience growth and understanding of our journeys in fleeting glimpses rather than in dramatic turning points. Truth unfolds slowly more often than it appears in great flashes of light. Its pattern remains hidden beneath the routine events of the day. Even if hope tells us our lives have a different direction and a destiny, it's only in gifted moments that we gain enough perspective to see this mosaic of meaning.

An ancient Orphic hymn proclaims that the night is the birth of all things. January takes us out into the bitter cold. Yet for Jorden's parents and for his doctor, the darkness of January was not a night of despair only but also a night of watching for the light that begins to emerge in January. They came to realize that in life as in death, we are truly linked together by a most fragile thread. Creation and compassion give birth to this delicate link. Gratitude and hope sustain it.

Consider This: When Loss or Death Happens

Many positive and downright inspirational events can push life in a new direction. Sometimes it's simply a need for a new challenge or a new lifestyle. Other times, an empty nest, an exciting promotion, or a move to a new state serves as a catalyst for change. Yet while we greet many major life changes with optimism, others come to us by way of loss or death.

The prospect of moving through such painful events or accompanying another person who has lost someone to death can be both difficult and frightening. None of us comes fully prepared to face grief; in fact, most of us come ill prepared and tend to stumble, despite our best intentions. There are no easy recipes or formulas, and each situation is unique. However, with a little thought and care, anyone can contribute in a positive way to troubling circumstances.

Perhaps most important, show up. Forget the idea that this person does not want to be bothered at such a miserable time. Once you choose to be with that person, begin by quietly listening and letting pain be pain, without trying to fix it.

When you or someone you know has been bereaved or has received a life-threatening diagnosis, the presence of a friend can produce a number of healing effects. Each of us can help to move another toward healing and assist him in looking toward the future when we

- avoid intellectualizing;
- let pain be pain;
- are prepared to listen and admit that we have no answers;
- offer a message that he does not have to go through this crisis alone;
- enable her to begin grieving in helpful ways;
- accept without judgment the full range of emotional responses;
- support him in making meaningful connections with others; and
- help her get back into simple routines.

6

Rekindle Your Celestial Light

*I will love the light for it shows me the way, yet I will endure
the darkness
because it shows me the stars.*
—Og Mandino

The day inevitably arrives when we find ourselves asking, "Why? Why didn't I settle down in a sensible job and make sensible contributions to a 401(k)? Where was the lemon law when I launched my search for a life partner? Why am I now sitting at home on a Friday night knitting a sweater for the dog? What happened to that zippy self that once embraced life with such verve? Come to think of it, what happened to that old spark that kept me out there, making an effort to contribute?"

The truth is, it makes no sense to think that life would glide along on a perfectly predictable path when everything and everyone around us continues to change. Yet our culture propagates this myth that says we deserve happiness, and if we run into a rough patch or have to recalculate our plan along the way, it must be our own doing. This is the time to remember that chastising oneself or others for tossing a wrench in the works doesn't help anything. What does help is rediscovering our strengths and virtues and evaluating where they might be best applied in the future.

For all the friends and acquaintances who have asked me, "Where is that divine light hiding in my time of need?" I offer the following story I wrote for a young teen recovering from anorexia nervosa:

Long ago, one deep, dark night, a small party of powerful gods met to discuss a frightening revelation—a threat of such scale that it endangered their very survival as gods. It seemed that while they had been reclining upon their ample backsides, boasting of their admirable achievements, a rumor began circulating among the mortals. The rumor claimed that they, mere mortals, also held the potential for divinity. Deeply disturbed at this career-threatening breakthrough, the gods made haste to convene a blue-ribbon task force to study the matter.

The impressive guest list said it all. Fertility gods, war gods, sports gods, celebrity gods—every majestic mover and supreme shaker whose reputation stood to suffer from this looming disaster received a summons.

The meeting day arrived, and delegates of every celestial order appeared. First came registration and refreshments ... a bit of small talk. Quickly, however, the standard networking gave way to a clamorous cacophony framed by one burning question:

"What are we going to do about these ungrateful boors who call themselves mortals?"

"Who do they think they are?" snorted an irritable investment god. "For years I've heard nothing but whine, whine, whine. 'Buy this.' 'Sell that.' 'Maybe mutual funds.' 'No, make it wheat futures.' I can't remember when they haven't been making some kind of demand. Now it looks as if they want to compete with us, for heaven's sake. They might be tiresome to work with, but if mortals ever do find this divine spark, I could be out of business. We all could be standing in the royal unemployment lines!"

"You're absolutely right!" roared a defense god. "A discovery like this could spell supremely slashed budgets and heavenly hiring freezes. Why, imagine what would happen if they figured out how to get along without us ...

or with each other, gods forbid! You know the old chestnut, 'No bombs, no budgets.' That means downsized operations. Maybe even enforced retirements. If this spark gets out of the bag, we can say good-bye golf games and hello quality improvement consultants."

"Well, for Pete's sake, we need to settle down and figure out where on earth we can hide the spark of divinity so that mortals never get their hands on it."

Ideas swirled about the conference hall, wild and complicated schemes. Gods whose social paths rarely crossed now huddled together, oddly linked through a common fear for their future security. What a throng of stewing sovereigns they made.

Unfortunately, their rank outshone their cleverness, for none came up with a solution on which the others could agree.

"Upstarts," grumbled a football deity. "They have no idea just how tricky this god business can be when it lands in the wrong hands."

Everyone nodded, appreciative of his discerning insight.

The day passed with no sign of a solution. Twilight seeped across the frozen landscape. Currents of life retired to their silent roots, waiting for winter or at least some solution to the immediate crisis. The gods mused. Beleaguered congressional delegates reconvened, pinch-faced and pale, to tick off a lackluster list of ideas upon which nobody could agree.

"How about hiding that spark of divinity in an oyster at the bottom of the sea?" offered one. "Or perhaps in a distant galaxy, just to make sure that nobody benefits from it?"

"No, no, no," growled an IRS god. "Why, in no time, some dopey diver or astronaut will discover it and steal it away or post on Twitter."

"How about inside a smoldering volcano?" proposed another.

"Or in an osprey's nest high upon a mountain peak?" advised a third. "Perhaps among the bunchberries that carpet the forest floor?"

Disapproving murmurs followed each suggestion. At last they gave up and prepared to adjourn and go home. Just then, an elderly woman, a Hearthkeeper, so they said, raised her hand tentatively.

"What is it?" demanded the chief executive god, who by this time had a migraine and wanted to go home. "Speak up, madam."

The Hearthkeeper rose to her feet with a certain grace and rather floated to the front of the conference hall. Far less flamboyant than the other delegates, she wore a simple woolen tunic with a linen shawl about her shoulders. With her silver hair secured in an amber clasp, she was a bit of a mystery. Most of the other gods found her slightly peculiar, as she always seemed preoccupied with small kindnesses. Though none of the gods had ever actually caught her speaking to a mortal, some suspected her of giving away trade secrets.

The woman whispered her proposal to the chief executive god. He brightened slightly. Normally, he would have dismissed a Hearthkeeper's idea as a time-waster, but he had nothing better to offer. Besides, he was in a hurry to get home for supper.

So he shared her idea with his assistant, who actually laughed out loud with delight. The gloom lifted noticeably from the room as one by one, the guests passed the Hearthkeeper's suggestion all around. Nonetheless, even in their excitement, they spoke in a whisper for fear that some gate-crashing mortal might overhear.

"It's perfect," crowed the defense god jubilantly. "Why, even heat-seeking missiles couldn't find it there. No one will capture that old spark of divinity now. We need never again contend with those brazen folks overstepping their authority."

With that, the delegates voted unanimously in favor of the Hearthkeeper's idea and then departed from the convention.

A year later, in the month of December, two men plodded along a dark and lonely road in the northern territory. They walked without words, staring sadly at the night sky. Snow drifted about their feet in soft meringue peaks. Disillusioned and brokenhearted, they leaned into the wind. The winter landscape lay unadorned except by a frozen sky. They heard no music beyond the bitter wind. The night bore them only icy tears. They had been searching for a divine spark, but tonight they abandoned hope. Now, the men simply longed for home and a warm fire.

An elderly woman stood alone at the roadside where they walked. Bundled in a simple woolen tunic, she watched from beneath her shawl. The travelers moved slowly, driving themselves onward with thoughts of a warm hearth. When they came within hearing distance, she called to them pleasantly.

"Who are you, and what brings you out on such a night as this?"

"We're weary mortals," called the younger man through the darkness. "We've been searching. We have combed the valleys and hillsides, convinced that we would find a divine spark, a light of implication."

"But why do you seek such a light?" queried the woman.

"Because we have become impoverished by our affluence and broken by our own powerlessness," lamented the older man. "We hunger for hope and yearn for reconciliation. We are overburdened by tension and confused by the world's empty promises. We need such a light to show us the way."

The woman inquired further, "What makes you think this divine spark exists? And tell me, too, what would you do with it, should you find it?"

The older man continued his bitter treatise, as if he hadn't heard her. "Snow falls now on our path. We have watched the skies for signs. We have wandered the roads of our past, questioning what we might have done differently to lead us to this wondrous spark. We have traveled through streets of violence and oppression in hope of kindling a new flame in our hearts. We hoped for inspiration and peace."

The woman reached out to receive their sorrow and pressed it to her heart. Then she asked if they would accompany her to her hearth. The exhausted and freezing men agreed, and the three set off together into the night of discovery.

"Do you know that night is the birth of all things?" the woman asked her two companions. "Night wears a mantle of snow; it watches and waits. Winter is a waiting season and a time of breakthroughs."

The men listened but did not understand. They walked in silence until they came to the woman's hut. She invited them in to warm by her fire and refresh themselves.

"Break bread with me," she implored. "Let your strength return before you continue your search."

Inside the hut, encircled by warmth, the travelers accepted a bit of cheese and hot tea from the woman while they dried their clothes near her fire. Her simple cottage boosted their spirits, a cozy respite from their burdens and the cold.

Meanwhile, the woman busied herself preparing a parcel of food, which she wrapped in her linen shawl. She helped the men into their coats and wished them well as they set out for home.

"This should see you through the night," she said, handing them the small bundle. "Blessings on you and yours," she called behind them as they disappeared into the blackness.

Near dawn, the men came to a small village. Exhausted from fighting the wind and snow, they took shelter in a barn. They settled themselves into a mound of straw and thought about the strange woman. They thought also about their failed search for the spark of divinity.

"We have not accomplished anything that we set out to do," the older man sighed. "All the good intentions. All the dreams and plans. All our hopes for success have failed. It just doesn't seem fair."

In the midnight hour, they contemplated the events of the past months. At last the young man pulled the woman's bundle from beneath his coat to see what she had given them to eat. He laid the contents upon the straw to share with his friend. The contents included a piece of cheese, a loaf of bread, some dried apples, and a few hazelnuts. Beneath the food was an envelope, secured by an amber clasp.

They ate, while the older man removed the amber clasp and opened the envelope. He examined the single piece of parchment and read it to his friend:

> Break this bread and think of me
> A sage who's lived enough to see
> That peace and fairness and love are real
> For those who listen, forgive, and feel
> Who know how to laugh and know how to grieve
> And celebrate life, both its pain and reprieve.
>
> To you who have searched every place far and near
> You now need to know that there's nothing to fear
> For all that is well will be well from now on
> With you who have wandered and struggled anon
> For lo, as you looked everywhere for the spark
> The light that you seek lives deep in your heart.

Consider This: Exploring the Meaning of Success

The characters in this tiny tale see their efforts as failure. What does success mean to you? It certainly wears countless faces. Achievements. Affluence. Acquisitions. Awards.

And those just begin with the letter A! While each of these can enhance the quality of our lives, they do not dig deeply into the meaning of success. In fact, a teen recovering from anorexia would express an entirely different view of success than a business leader accepting a new position as CEO. In order to travel the road you desire, it's essential to first define or redefine your own vision of success, according to what best suits you, not what aligns with contemporary culture's vision. In broadening the meaning of success, it helps to start small. Consider your daily experience of work, interpersonal relationships, and play by asking yourself the following:

- What three things bring me the most—though perhaps simplest—joy?
- What, outside of work, engenders feelings of accomplishment?
- Beyond specific achievements, what fosters my self-esteem?
- On a scale of one to ten, how would I rate my level of success?

7

Tom Warth Lets His Inspiration Speak

*Start by doing what's necessary; then do what's possible;
and suddenly you are doing the impossible.*
—Francis of Assisi

He came to the United States in 1960, a restless, twenty-four-year-old British immigrant, searching for more enticing work than his father's construction company offered.

"I didn't want to work for my dad," said long-time automotive book publisher Tom Warth. "Defying one's parents in the 1950s was not an easy choice, but I was curious and wanted to see America."

Fifty-five years later, Tom has traveled the world and worked his way through more than one plan before arriving at a perfect role for him: that of an inspired humanitarian.

It began when his family met an American serviceman based at a US Air Force facility near their Cambridge, England, home. The new friend, Hal Hall, eventually offered to sponsor Tom as an immigrant and invited him to come live with the Hall family in Eau Claire, Wisconsin. Tom seized the opportunity and set out for America, confident that he would discover every measure of exciting prospects.

When he arrived at the Halls' Wisconsin home, he found a job at a local drugstore, bought a car, and eventually drove around the country. His first American grand tour ended up in New Orleans, where he took in the 1961 Mardi Gras. Soon afterward, he loaded his Volkswagen on a boat and returned to England to marry his sweetheart, Ursula. The newlyweds returned to the United States shortly after the wedding. This time, Tom recommended they settle in Minneapolis, where he went to work for Prudential Insurance. He had yet to meet his goal of self-employment.

"I worked for Prudential for five years," said Tom. "I was always trying to find a niche. This led me to buying and selling old cars, including a Rolls-Royce that once belonged to poet Rudyard Kipling."

Soon Tom's old-car enterprise turned to British car magazines. He eventually started purchasing books from England rather than from American publishers. Meanwhile, the Warth home was filling up with books, and Tom was beginning to believe that this little start-up company of his might just work.

"I realized that my audience would buy specific car magazines and books, not because they liked books but because they wanted information about specific cars," he explained. "At some point, things were going so well that I bought an ad in *Road and Track* magazine."

He also decided to leave Prudential and finally follow his dream of working for himself. The move produced predictable reactions from those close to him. His father reminded him of the horrors of the Great Depression and, by the way, did his son know that most new businesses failed? Tom's boss reproached him for considering such a whimsical idea, insisting he was foolish to leave Prudential. Tom ignored the nagging from colleagues and family, tapped into his characteristic optimism and, a few years later, ended up hiring the once-reproachful Prudential boss.

The next step in his grand plan involved building a new business home in tiny Osceola, Wisconsin. Here, he watched his fledgling Classic Motorbooks, Inc. grow at an impressive pace. His annual sale and open houses became legend and soon ballooned into a bigger party called Wheels and Wings. It included car and airplane shows and became a destination of car collectors and enthusiasts throughout the region. His business became dominant in the automotive publishing field worldwide. Tom prospered and, at the perfect moment, sold Classic Motorbooks to the *San Francisco Chronicle*.

"We used to say we didn't want to grow more than 15 percent a year," he explained, "but we were growing quickly." He hired expert talent from England and at one point had as many as a hundred employees, plus a few managers who didn't get along with one another.

"I wasn't the best boss, because I couldn't seem to fire anybody, even the troublesome ones," he admitted.

After the sale of Motorbooks, he kept his toe in the publishing world by maintaining an out-of-print business. Meanwhile, since the Motorbooks sale included a no-compete restriction, Tom found himself free to explore the infinite list of possibilities for his next adventure.

"When I sold the business, I wanted to take the money and invest it where it would make a real difference," said Tom.

That was when he met Loy Zabasajja, a Ugandan woman visiting her children in the United States. Since he had been cut loose from the responsibility of running a business, he asked Loy if he could come to visit her in Uganda.

"She agreed, though I'm not sure she believed I'd really show up," said Tom. "I like adventure, and the best places to find it are remote spots with no tourists but where you know someone." Loy's hometown of Jinja, Uganda, made a perfect destination for a man researching his next big plan.

Upon his arrival in Kampala, Uganda's capital city, he took a memorable bus ride to the home of his new friend Loy. In Tom's words, it escalated to a breathtaking bus-driver duel when his driver challenged another to a race though the countryside. Surprisingly, they made it to Jinja unscathed, though he chose to continue his Ugandan tour on foot. It was in Jinja, when Loy walked with him to the local library, that he discovered a building equipped with a librarian, plenty of bookshelves and children waiting to learn, but no books.

Suddenly, this inspired humanitarian saw that it was time to take action.

"I realized we had so many books in America, and I had many publishing contacts," said Tom. "So I went home and pitched my idea to a group of publishers, booksellers, and librarians who made up the Minnesota Book Publishers' Roundtable."

Eventually, a handful of book lovers from this diverse group joined with Tom to create what would become Books for Africa. To some, it might have seemed like a simple idea to reclaim good books destined for landfills and put them into the hands of African children. To those children, who have since received thirty-three million good books, the results have been profound. With a mission of ending the book famine in Africa, Books for Africa helps create a culture of literacy and the empowerment tools to support it.

The premise is straightforward. Books donated by publishers, schools, libraries, individuals, and organizations come to a warehouse, where volunteers carefully sort and chose age- and subject-appropriate books. They then pack the books for shipping in large sea containers, paid for by contributions.

"It costs about fifty cents to send a book from the United States to Africa," said Tom. That book will get read by fifty children, which brings the cost of reaching one child with a book to one penny—one penny to impact a child's life. I can't think of any better investment of a person's philanthropic money."

Books for Africa volunteers have shipped books to forty-nine different countries since 1988. Over a twelve-month period in 2014, the organization has shipped some two and a half million books, valued at thirty-five million dollars, to twenty-seven African countries. Add to that 223 computers and eleven new law and human rights libraries. Yet Tom doesn't take this success for granted.

"We pat ourselves on the back for our accomplishment, but there are over five hundred million children in Africa," he adds. "We are the largest shipper of books to Africa from the Western world. No one else sells or donates as many books as we do. But there is much more to be done, and we are continually working."

Thirty-three million books sent to a country with half a billion children can make the work seem impossible, so Tom brightens the journey with long, invitational, consciousness-raising walks. So far, he has covered many miles, as close as Wisconsin's Ice Age Trail and as far away as the "Million Books for Gambia" walk across that tiny African country.

Recently, Books for Africa stepped in to help provide needed books for children of Liberia, kept at home from school in an effort to contain the spread of the deadly Ebola virus.

"Books are about ideas. Books are stories. Books are about people," explained Ahmed Sirleaf, a US embassy advisor in Monrovia, Liberia. Sirleaf grew up in Liberia and recalled the benefit of reading American books as a child. "To send twenty-two thousand books to Liberia at this point in time, particularly after the Ebola crisis, is timely and will change lives," he added.

"The population of Africa is currently estimated at one billion, and half are children," said Tom. "Two generations have grown up with our books. When we sent our first load of books, I was surprised at how much good it could do. I think people don't realize how much we can do with so little."

If Tom Warth is any example of that, he came to this country with nothing, but chose to be a contributor, an innovator, and a dreamer. My guess is most of us possess these and other assets that can help us to our next big adventure. The question is, do we say yes or no when the opportunity appears before us?

Consider This: Positive Psychology and the Art of Saying Yes

Tom Warth exemplifies a variety of assets studied within the field of positive psychology, which involves the scientific observation of human flourishing and an applied approach to optimal functioning. It has sometimes been defined as the study of the strengths and virtues that enable individuals, communities, and organizations to thrive.

Positive psychology originates in the belief that people want to lead meaningful and fulfilling lives, to cultivate what is best within them, and to enhance their experiences of love, work, and play.

Four of the major tenets of positive psychology include:

- Rise to life's challenges, and make the most of setbacks and adversity.
- Engage and relate to other people.
- Find fulfillment in creativity and productivity.
- Look beyond self and help others to find lasting meaning, satisfaction, and wisdom.
  —Positive Psychology Institute;
  positivepsychologyistitute.com.au

8

The Upside of Doubt and Questioning

Never doubt that a small group of thoughtful, committed citizens can change the world; indeed, it's the only thing that ever has.
—Margaret Mead

Each passing year brings more communication clutter into my space. Some mornings I stare at my computer, trying to remember just when I fell into the grip of Twitter, text messaging, and happy-hour networking. Not that I'm adept at any of these. But for a woman who began her career with an IBM Selectric typewriter on her desk, I do spend an inordinate amount of time trying to keep up to speed. And some days I doubt the health benefits offered up by this daily immersion into communication technology,

Yes, the number and strength of social connections provides an essential piece of our well-being, and information technology plays a vital role. However, years of listening to people who wrestle with loss and setbacks tell me we need something more than Instagram or e-mail to keep in touch. During seasons of doubt, we can easily become dangerous weapons against ourselves, especially if we choose to spend too much time alone, bingeing on last season's *Game of Thrones* or texting friends while hunkered down over a frozen pizza.

Isolation, like heresy, begins with a thread of truth and stretches it into untruth. It can turn from a contemplative treasure to poison. In fact, people recovering from addiction often say that every time they feel a need to isolate themselves from others, they know that what they really want is a drink. The line between solitude and isolation is a fine one.

Isolation invites self-absorption and self-centeredness. When we set out to get away from those who bother us or make our lives complicated, we lose our objectivity. We start to deceive ourselves, get our priorities mixed up and, in the words of my astute father, "We attempt to fool a damn good person."

I suspect that one reason we sometimes avoid the community of others is that we are afraid someone might tell us something we suspect is true but would rather deny. Community, after all, consists of a body of shared truths. That body of truths has a unique way of maintaining a more genuine honesty than any individual assertions of truth can possibly attain.

The relationship between helplessness and doubt is much like that between isolation and solitude. While unattended helplessness can lead to gratuitous self-pity or stuck-in-the-mud imprisonment, doubt involves movement. It implies that something will eventually get resolved.

One could say that doubt's most vital function is that it compels us to find answers. Doubt ultimately demands the truth. When in doubt, it's hard to simply flounder about indefinitely without taking any kind of action. One look at the development of our technical civilization since the time of the Enlightenment says it all. It has been built on doubt. Enormous achievements in medicine have come about because someone doubted someone else's previous methods. Doubt has pushed us forward into vast new frontiers of knowledge.

Think of the discoveries and events of recent history that are founded in doubt. We have come to doubt the viability of nuclear war. We doubt that our earth can hold up much longer under the ecological siege we have put to her. We doubt that business and industry know how to responsibly look after the environment. We doubt that assault rifles comprise a necessary commodity for hunters, or that blind faith in any government or religion is a sound idea.

These kinds of doubts can actually turn us around and invite us to step up to a different truth. By pulling us toward a higher level of consciousness and maturity, doubts awaken new sensitivity. Good things can and do emerge from doubting, as was the case with a physician friend of mine who developed colon cancer at the peak of an illustrious career in which he doubted much and discovered plenty.

A neonatologist who began caring for critically ill newborns when the field had just begun to emerge, Stephen treated medicine as an adventure filled with thrilling possibilities. He became a pioneer, working in a newborn intensive care unit with sick and prematurely born infants. At times he would retreat to his laboratory, where he searched for better techniques to treat tiny preemies with underdeveloped lungs. He lectured. He taught throughout the United States, Europe, and Japan. He enjoyed enormous success, though he would not have described success in conventional terms. Stephen found his success by questioning the status quo. He became a chronic doubter whose bold changes in treatment technology ultimately saved the lives of thousands of infants and won the respect of their families.

Stephen always had a clear view of who he was and what he wanted to accomplish as a physician. Patient care meant everything to him, and although he constantly dealt with lives in the balance, he maintained a sense of silliness and levity. This included shaving his head as a gesture of solidarity with bald newborns or babies in chemotherapy. It also included opinionated outbursts during tedious hospital leadership meetings.

"There are people who care too much about the human condition and not enough about the Minnesota Twins," he proclaimed on more than one occasion. "It's so easy to get caught up in the details and miss the great drama of being alive."

He knew how to focus on what was important and, at

the same time, enjoy the rest of the world around him. A man with strong opinions about patient care, Stephen once found himself in the middle of an insurance company/hospital dispute concerning who was going to pay for what. It seemed that a hospitalized baby with chronic health problems was generating a large medical bill that the family's insurance company refused to pay. Nobody really knew if the baby could stay in the hospital any longer or would have to be moved to an alternative setting. Finally, at some critical point in the argument, Stephen summed up his sentiments to the squabbling parties:

"If he goes, I go."

The baby stayed.

On another occasion, a letter he received from a sixth-grader he had treated years earlier produced the same quick response from Stephen. The letter began, "Hi, I don't know if anyone remembers me ..."

Stephen immediately wrote back: "We do remember you. You were a very small, very sick baby, one of the first patients to receive a new therapy ... Many people think doctors and nurses are different, that we don't feel the same things other people feel. That's not true ... we are just ordinary people working in somewhat extraordinary jobs. Your letter reminded us of how wonderfully extraordinary our jobs really are."

The word "ecstasy" originates in the Greek *ekstasis*, which derives from *ek*, meaning out, and *stasis*, a state of standstill. In other words, to be ecstatic means to be outside of a fixed place. We can recognize those who live ecstatic lives because they are always moving away from static situations. They are the doubtful and the restless explorers who always hunt for unmapped territory to investigate. An ecstatic person thrives on doubt, knowing that uncertainty and skepticism precede the discovery of truth and, perhaps, an exciting new plan.

Stephen exemplified the ecstatic person who lives in a place where determination constantly breaks through the walls of uncertainty. When he chose to live ecstatically, he chose a shared life, a life in community with others who also allowed themselves to doubt and question and to learn with him. He left the safe and familiar place of rigid medical beliefs and pat solutions and reached out to others as he cared for sick and dying children. He ventured onto untilled soil, even when it involved risking a journey into someone else's suffering. Ecstasy such as the kind Stephen championed always reaches out to new freedom, including freedom from oppression, injustice, and ignorance.

Conversely, static living separates us and transforms us into self-absorbed beings, fighting for our own individual survival. Ecstatic living brings us together to discover one another, to be responsible for one another, and to proclaim life as creative and filled with potential.

As Stephen became increasingly ill, he often talked about the meaning of his work. "I'm so happy to have had a job that made a difference, to feel a sense of purpose," he would say. "How incredible it's been to be invited into people's lives at such critical junctures—to walk with them and know them. Sometimes people would come up and thank me for something I had done years ago, or tell me how well their child was doing. Sometimes students would do the same. You just never know when you might discover something new or influence someone's life, even in a small way."

When I asked this restless, questioning, opinionated, politically incorrect, and dying medical adventurer what he wanted to tell the rest of us, he simply said, "Show up, listen, and tell the truth." Even at the end of his life, curiosity drove his clinical research and care standards, while his empathy for families helped ease the pain of their anxious vigils.

Finally, in a voice edged with something between humility and doubt, he added.

"I did the best I could … at least I think so."

Consider This: Compassion as the Ground for Healing and Well-Being

"Do we create or destroy?" asked Dag Hammarskjold in his classic *Markings*. Living out compassion is an act of creation and a priceless asset for the journey. If words like "love" and "compassion" have suffered from excess or misunderstanding, it might be because we have forgotten where they really belong. This whole experience that we call life is really a single lesson that lies at the heart of wholeness and well-being. That lesson begins with a question: "How do we care for ourselves and others as we travel the path we have chosen?"

We all possess healing skills or assets that we can share at any given moment with others and ourselves. These skills are simple but powerful: a quiet presence, a capacity to listen without judgment, and a posture of hospitality.

- Caring, considered as pulling from abundance rather than as ego-centered, implies the existence of some greater force than oneself.
- A healing role includes the recognition that social support, prayer, ritual, and other expressions of spirituality are significant dimensions in the dynamics of hope and healing. To mobilize these resources for oneself or on a friend's behalf is both essential and filled with potential.
- No matter what the loss, we must recognize the value of having one's questions about meaning and hope taken seriously by a caring community or person.
- Giving voice to despair and grief opens both the sufferer and the healer to unanticipated strength with which to endure or transcend crisis. It can give strength to those who live with chronic conditions as they renegotiate their paths to accommodate an unanticipated change in direction.
- Making and maintaining connections with friends and family might not always appeal to someone struggling with

a loss, but these connections ultimately play a critical role in one's transition to a new plan.

Doubting can put us in touch with all sorts of helpful information concerning our chosen or uninvited path. Consider the following questions; do they resonate with your current circumstances? Do they play a role in the plan you would like to have chosen but did not? Do they inform your future?

- What keeps you awake at night?
- When did you last feel "at home" with yourself?
- When did you last feel really alive?
- When was the last time you felt fully immersed in your situation?
- What do you yearn for?
- What do you hope for?
- What have you given up on?

9

A Search for Meaning

If there is meaning in life at all, then there must be meaning in suffering.

—Viktor E. Frankl

A colleague once told me that theology really wasn't meant to be an intellectual exercise practiced in seminaries and graduate schools. It was more a matter of faith seeking understanding. I encountered this epiphany several years ago when I met a couple whose dreams of starting out on a new path to a new life met with an impossible loss. Though this occurred some time ago when women ministers were just becoming a real presence in pastoral ministry, it struck me that many of the details and attitudes in the story could easily have happened today and will continue to happen until we engage in heartfelt dialogue with the *stranger* whose life differs vastly from our own.

It began with a message from the birth center late on a Friday afternoon, an hour before the shift changed. The social worker on duty had just interviewed the Robinson family and felt they might appreciate a chaplain's presence. Though the Robinsons did not belong to a local church, Mr. Robinson expressed curiosity about meeting a woman minister.

"Mom is nearly full term, and her baby has died," reported the social worker, highlighting some of the pertinent details in Mrs. Robinson's chart. "She also has three small children at home and probably suffers from serious psychiatric problems," she mumbled offhandedly. Maybe bipolar disorder, schizophrenia, or borderline personality disorder—or any of several other debilitating possibilities, she advised me. The woman's reaction to her baby's death seemed "flat," according to others present at the nursing station. Most of the staff agreed that Mrs. Robinson had been joking oddly and that she failed to grasp the meaning of what was taking place in her life and her body.

A discussion then ensued about Mrs. Robinson's intellectual competence. The staff had given her some printed material about grief and loss, though they couldn't tell if she understood any of it or even cared. Perhaps the loss of this child was a relief to her, given the fact that she had a brood of very young children at home. The nurses and case managers continued to speculate about the situation. An unspoken question underlined their discussion: "Why would the Robinsons continue to have children when Mrs. Robinson was so sick and she already had three youngsters under the age of six?"

I too wondered about the entire incident, as I observed the facial expressions of those around that denoted everything from bewilderment to sanctimonious disapproval.

"How about the baby's father?" I asked. "Is he here?"

He was.

According to the staff, Mr. Robinson was behaving strangely too. His strident voice and peculiar chatter made them uneasy. He dominated his wife, bossing her and hardly permitting her to answer questions for herself, according to one of the nurses. Troubling too were his constant references to what he called his wife's medical mismanagement. He clearly thought that this might have contributed to their baby's death, and his questions were having a chilling effect on the various health professionals engaged in his wife's care.

Yet a housekeeper outside Mrs. Robinson's room volunteered something a little different. She felt that though he was overbearing and odd, Mr. Robinson seemed quite supportive of his wife—very sympathetic and reassuring. In any case, a strong bond obviously existed between them.

As I listened to the cacophony of opinions about the couple, it struck me that they were just that—individual opinions reflecting individual preferences, experiences, and comfort levels. The final diagnosis: Mr. Robinson talked too much, and he was ... well, she was ... that is, they were *different.* The social worker nodded in agreement.

I soon discovered that the Robinsons were, indeed, different. They differed from me and from the rest of the staff in ways that hindered much meaningful contact. While the differences began at a racial level, they included profound social, cultural, educational, and financial contrasts. The Robinsons embodied what could have been described as a subculture of loss. The rest of us—white, middle-class, and educated—exemplified privilege beyond the Robinsons' experience. To my knowledge, I had never intentionally wielded power over others. Nothing in my upbringing or education gave me any training in seeing myself as an oppressor. In fact, social justice ranked high on my list of priorities, a core value that had shaped my vocational call. But I also knew that I spent most of my waking moments in the company of other whites, a relatively easy audience for me to identify and negotiate with. Rarely had I experienced obstacles or setbacks that I wasn't able to transcend with a little grit and know-how. In addition, I possessed a convenient bundle of provisions, tools that made my life palatable—a passport, a checkbook, credit cards, a home, a car that ran, health insurance and, most significant, choices. This kind of privilege had little to do with my good intentions. A lifetime of best intentions did not make me any less privileged in the eyes of the people I was about to meet.

Mr. Robinson greeted me loudly with a predictable remark about never before having met a lady preacher. A thin veneer of jolly chatter barely concealed his anxiety and confusion. It wasn't long before he got to the point of his concern.

"They say that our baby be dead for a long time," he announced, "maybe a month. Maybe it plans on risin' up like Lazarus! Do you think so, Reverend?"

He slapped his knee and, with a loud guffaw, beckoned to his wife, evidently granting her permission to chuckle with him over his ice-breaking joke. She lay quietly in the bed, staring out the window, uncommitted to a conversation of any type. Mr. Robinson veered from one unrelated topic to another, regaling me with stories about everything from his tour of duty in the US Army to the theology of Martin Luther.

I asked if they had friends I could call for them.

"No," he replied. "We keep pretty much to ourselves. I maybe leave the house to go to the grocery store, but I don't stay away long. We stick with each other and our kids most the time."

"How about family?" I pressed, hoping to identify someone who might lend support. Mr. Robinson's parents had died some time ago. Mrs. Robinson's mother lived in Arkansas and didn't have a telephone. Neither of them knew how to reach any other relatives.

"No, we don't need to call no family," said Mr. Robinson. "We can take care of this ourselves."

I learned that the Robinsons had left Arkansas six months earlier. They were heading for Canada to start a new life when their dilapidated car broke down on the freeway. A highway patrolman arrived and, upon discovering that they had no automobile insurance, collected a $300 fine from them. The encounter left the family broke and marooned in the Twin Cities. When we met, they had already moved several times in search of a safe neighborhood for their children.

"A baby always love you, you know. Like, I know that a baby needs me to take care of it. I like that, don't you? I'm scared," said Mrs. Robinson to neither her husband nor me.

"A lady preacher. Well now, ain't that something? It would be good if you stayed with my wife while she has that baby. You know, my sister lost a baby once. And my mama lost twins. Hell, we've lost a lot of children, now that I think 'bout it. Yes, you could be a comfort to her when she has that baby."

Loss of power. Loss of identity. Loss of life.

"Is there anyone you would like to see or anything I could do for you?" I asked. "I've never lost a child. I don't know what it's like to be who you are or where you are."

"That baby ain't never done nothin' wrong, has it? God is gonna welcome that baby, ain't he? 'Course he will. I know it couldn't be no other way. I mean, what's that baby ever done wrong anyhow? 'Course God is gonna do that."

Loss of dignity. Loss of dreams.

"You know, the other day I come out to get in the car and the horn started to honk. Just like that. It was the day my wife found out that the baby died. That darn horn be honking all the way downtown. People kep' lookin' at me, and I kep' holdin' my hands up in the air—like this—so they could see I wasn't doin' it myself. It was doin' it itself. Craziest thing I ever did see. I think maybe that baby's spirit was right in that car, don't you know? That be it. I know it. That baby's spirit was in that car, tellin' us it was gonna be just fine up there in heaven. Do you think so, Reverend?"

Loss of access. Loss of privacy. Loss of connection.

"Mr. Robinson, do you think the three of us could just hold hands for a few minutes?"

He struggled out of his chair and made his way to the bedside, where he took his wife's hand and then mine. We stood, wordless against a backdrop of fetal monitors and rush-hour traffic. Gripped by my own inadequacy, I offered a halting prayer of encouragement ... for all of us. Tears slowly slipped down Mr. Robinson's cheeks. Mrs. Robinson kept her silent vigil, seemingly trying to summon the courage to give birth to her lifeless child.

We tightened our grasps on one another's hands, a spontaneous gesture that found me at once understanding everything and nothing.

It was but a mere hesitation, a suspended moment in space, when the three of us said yes to a life briefly shared and broken. Silently, we acknowledged the fragile and precious thread that wove us together, balanced in time and creation, a merging of kindred spirits never to be separated by a world of human limitations and prejudice.

Consider This: Words We Use Matter

A key figure in a chaplain's world of hospitals is the stranger. Whether learning about someone's culture or belief system or supporting families as they tentatively explore life after loss, a hospital chaplain often finds himself or herself in new lands, working among strangers. We venture into the unknown together, away from the safety and comfort of what we know—or think we know. Faith and convictions get tested and redefined, bringing new courage, especially when a stranger shines a new light to help us see.

Parker J. Palmer, author, educator, and activist, describes the stranger as a bearer of truth that might not otherwise have been received. "We often need the stranger's line of vision to help us see straight," he explains. "For example, each of us has potentials and limitations that become invisible to us and to those near us; we cannot see the forest for the trees. But when the stranger comes along and looks at us afresh, without bias or preconception, those qualities may quickly become apparent"[1]—a startling truth that came to light the day I met the Robinson family.

Friends and relatives tend to feel helpless and inadequate when encountering those who have experienced a loss. Just remember that words of support and encouragement can contribute in a very helpful way to the healing process.

---

[1] Parker J. Palmer, *The Company of Strangers* (New York, NY: Crossroad, 1981), 44.

- Ask the person to tell her or his story and describe the events surrounding this loss.
- Acknowledge that you don't know exactly what she feels like.
- Ask if he wants you to call someone to be with him; encourage him to ask for help, and help him to make a list of what he needs from others.
- Ask if she needs more information to help her understand what has happened or to make decisions.
- Use honest and respectful words near to her experience, not abstract terms and euphemisms; help validate the person's feelings.
- Don't be afraid of awkward silence; your presence brings comfort, even without words.

10

Noah's Notes—Invent New Happiness Habits

So Gabe and I were enjoying a friendly round of cribbage one spring morning when Madam pulled up a chair, sat down with a thud, and sighed deeply.

"It's time for some resolutions," she muttered.

"You're late," replied Gabe without looking up. He continued to deal me a new hand. "We celebrated the new year three months ago," he added. "Besides that, we horses are kind of averse to a bunch of tedious decrees that begin with *no.*"

"Perhaps you should be conducting this conversation with Henri le Chat Noire," I offered delicately. "Now there's a clever cat who has parlayed tedium and ennui into a fine career."

"No, no, that's not it," exclaimed Madam. "I'm talking about my wardrobe and my weight." She snorted and then groaned. "And what about this hairdo that just spent a long winter under a Carhartt hat? Good grief, if we intend to go to the Erma Bombeck Writers' Workshop next month, I'll need a serious fashion tune-up."

It was a reasonable observation on her part.

"And how would you like to begin your fashion-forward makeover?" I asked the woman who still operated a Lady Kenmore washer and a 1952 reel lawnmower.

"That's why I'm here," she retorted. "I need your advice."

Gabe folded his cards and waited for something brilliant to spring from my lips.

"Um ... maybe we should add a cheery twist to this plan of yours," I proposed. "How about a *happiness habit* approach rather than a *Debbie Downer* one?"

She surveyed her flannel-lined jeans and size-ten Muck Boots and shot me a disbelieving glance. "But I—"

"In fact, let's plan that happiness assignment we've been talking about for months," I interrupted before she could protest. "It would call for resolutions of a more appealing nature. So, for example, you could whip up a slimming kale smoothie in the interest of weight management, while I enter my Twenty-Four-Karat Cake in the Pillsbury Bakeoff. We might want to call that a *Spread the Joy* resolution."

Gabe rolled his eyes and opened up his *Wall Street Journal*.

"Next, you might consider recycling those stylish sweat pants of yours as cleaning rags, and I'll dump my winter-fragrant Rambo blanket in the trash bin," I offered. "That strikes me as a *Lighten Up* resolution."

"I'm not sure that's what lighten up means, but I do see some potential in your approach," she admitted.

A few days later, Madam and I began noodling something novel—a themed road trip. We would call it our First Annual Happiness Habits Party, to be exact. She brightened at my idea, and I noticed she had already ditched the baseball cap and visited her hair stylist, Kelly, at Aveda for a decent color and cut. Things looked promising.

"Surely this will be more fun than a gluten-free diet and much more relaxing than our project last year—the chuck-wagon trail ride through Montana's rattlesnake country," I added. She agreed.

So I dusted off the Rand McNally Road Atlas, and we chose a more manageable destination—Ely, Minnesota. Ely serves as home to North Pole dogsled explorer extraordinaire, Will Steger. Given Will's setting of a high bar, Ely seemed like a perfect starting point to launch some of our grand happiness habits. Plus, rattlesnakes hate Ely because the temperature gets down to forty-some degrees below zero in the winter.

Madam decided to invite a couple of her friends, Stephanie and Miss Vicki, to join us. Since the trip honored our first happiness habit resolution, *Just Say Yes*, she also invited the Terrific Terriers, Winnie and Bear, plus her Fluff Muffin cat.

For readers unfamiliar with the Boundary Waters Canoe Area, Ely is situated near Lake One, approximately three rest stops and one terrier throw-up north of Saint Paul. That, combined with Madam's checkered success operating her GPS, made it a longish drive. However, five hours in the car and the Fluff Muffin's erratic use of his litter box provided ample opportunity for the three women to exercise happiness habit resolution number two, *Let It Go*.

That's when *The Happiness Project* author, Gretchen Rubin, came to mind. No doubt she would have approved of our third new habit, *Spread the Joy*. It fit nicely into the birthday celebration we held in honor of Stephanie's Medicare moment. Not only did the party include a fabulous soufflé cake and two bottles of chardonnay, but it also transformed the occasion into a festive AARP enterprise. That transition took place when the *girl* talk veered sharply from attractive men they had met to high-fiber food.

Post-party, night one, cabin seventeen—the foursome washed up their party dishes, tidied the cabin, and tucked themselves into their cozy futons. This all took place by nine bells. Then, sometime after midnight, a woodland creature attempted to enter the cabin through an open window. Apparently the women thought the sound came from a bear, because all four reacted as if a tornado siren had gone off. Madam started shouting safety instructions and waved a canister of Mace pepper spray that she mistook for a flashlight. The terriers barked bravely. All the while, the Fluff Muffin paid little attention to the rumpus in the living room. Instead, he leisurely reclined on the kitchen counter, entertaining a small field mouse. The terrified creature was attempting to transport an M&M chocolate bar to his abode behind the refrigerator.

Unfortunately for the mouse, the candy wrapper made a fearsome crackling sound that awoke the cat and sent the women into bear alert.

This memorable scene came to a end when, in the interest of happiness habit number four, *Be More Inclusive,* Madam chased the cat away and prepared a plate of *quiet* food for the mouse. The M&M candy wrapper had to go, but the tiny intruder could now enjoy a midnight snack of peanut butter and jelly without waking the domestic pets and intrepid campers.

So the weekend unfolded with less midnight activity and more excellent contributions to Madam's and my happiness-habits research. In short, our up-North cabin party scored well on improving our attitudes, particularly when it came to field-mouse hospitality.

11

Nourishing the Body Can Feed the Soul

Eating with the fullest pleasure is perhaps the profoundest enactment of our connection with the world. In this pleasure we experience and celebrate our dependence and our gratitude.
—Wendell Berry

Michelle, longtime neighbor, met me for coffee and, during the course of our catching up, shared a story about her son Andrew. I knew Andrew had struggled with his share of problems, though I did not know he had come home to live with his mother after a ten-year absence. A once-magnificent athlete and promising musician, this gifted young man had abandoned college only to tumble headlong into a mire of drugs and despair. His family watched, powerless, as he continued his free fall toward a frightening abyss.

That morning, Michelle offered many more details about a torturous decade of Andrew's misadventures: drunk-driving arrests, motorcycle wrecks, ruined friendships, lost employment, late-night phone calls, threatened suicide, and multiple attempts by his family to get help for him. Creditors' letters arrived, demanding delinquent payments. Complete strangers called to express concern for his safety. All who knew Andrew held their collective breath, waiting for the worst. Many tried to intervene. Many more gave in or gave up. Andrew rejected every invitation to reclaim his life.

Finally, one day, for no clear reason, he simply came to his mother's home. Perhaps he knew something better awaited him there. Maybe he grasped, ever so dimly, the consequence of traveling further down the path he had chosen for himself. More than likely he just ran out of money and places to hide. The reason for his return hardly mattered to his mother. He showed up at her kitchen door one morning, and that was all that counted.

"His empty gaze startled me," said Michelle. "Everything about him seemed out of sync and out of touch."

She described feeling strangely uneasy, sitting close to him at the kitchen table, being alone in the house with him. Pale and empty, he displayed not a hint of the joyful child who grew up in her home. Where had he been all this time? Who had he become? How might she care for him and help restore him to some semblance of health? Was there any hope of awakening him to better choices and a new life path? If his return home signaled a new opportunity, how would they find success together, as a community of two?

They sat in relative silence, she maneuvering gingerly around the missing years. A virtual stranger looked back at her from across the kitchen table. Her thoughts tumbled. All she knew about addiction and "tough love" seemed unsuitable for this occasion. She groped for helpful insight. The counselors never told her what was supposed to happen next. So she waited in clumsy silence for some profound piece of wisdom to surface. Nothing did. At last, guided only by intuition and love, she got up from her chair, kissed Andrew, and went to the kitchen stove to prepare him breakfast. For the next year, she quite literally fed him back to health.

Food wields a mighty power. It provides comfort to heart, body, and soul. Food serves as a universal language. It connects us one to another, even when other familiar avenues of connection have closed. And of course, food connects one to another as a source of celebration and joy!

The day Michelle let go of trying to fix Andrew and began cooking with intention for her wounded son, she somehow infused his meals with that loving kindness. By preparing food and eating with him for the next several months, she offered him sustaining energy and power of life. Partaking in the gift of food implicated her in her son's struggle for recovery. It brought her into community with him and created an intimacy that might never have been achieved otherwise. The food she provided fed both his body and his soul. In the midst of confusion she instinctively created a nourishing environment in which she could support him as he recovered his personhood and considered a new direction in life.

In studying the food-related beliefs of various wisdom traditions, nutritionist Deborah Kesten discovered that honoring food through thoughtful preparation and then partaking of it with depth and sincerity actually makes it sacred. Food is sanctified by warmth and affection. She found that many traditions offer a spiritual perspective that we have forgotten over the centuries. When we furnish food with such sacred understanding, it nourishes both body and spirit. When we appreciate food in this manner, we also contribute in an essential way to healing.[2]

Most cultures and religions have rituals that use food as a means of connecting to a deeper spiritual significance. Jewish dietary laws, for example, honor the sanctity of the life inherent in both animal- and plant-based food. Christians sustain their connection to Jesus Christ through the bread and wine of Holy Communion. African Americans season their soul food with love as a way of celebrating community and friendships. Yogis eat, in part, to commune with food's life-giving qualities, while Muslims honor food for its divine essence. Buddhists pursue enlightenment by bringing a meditative awareness to food. The Chinese communicate with

---

[2] Deborah Kesten, *Feeding the Body, Nourishing the Soul* (Berkeley, Calif.: Conari Press, 1997).

the gods through food, and the Japanese turn to tea to renew the spirit.[3]

While food as spiritual sustenance enjoys a rich history in countless cultures, traditional nutritional science has, in recent history, been based primarily on biology. Nutritional science has attempted to understand, explain, or control the content of our food and in this way has provided an incomplete picture, based on a particular worldview. Food has been viewed mainly as a collection of nutrients—fuel for the body that could be measured and adjusted. Nutritional scientists learned to break down foods into proteins, fats, carbohydrates, and minerals. The calorie, a measure of food energy established by the French chemist Antoine Laurent Lavoisier in the eighteenth century, added to the measurement tools.

Even in today's growing Slow Food movement and preponderance of websites and authors like Michael Pollan exploring the meaning of food, popular media demonstrates how diet and nutrition continue to reflect this mechanistic approach. Diet and health publications remain preoccupied with measuring the contents of food. Our focus on calories, fat content, and how cooking and processing change the nutrient value of food reveals that we still treat food as the fuel that runs or clogs various human body parts. Vitamins, minerals, energy drinks, and all manner of food supplements drive the body and tune up our physical and intellectual performances. Our seemingly more balanced approach to nutrition still breaks the body down into separates—heart, brain, or colon— with each part requiring a specific nutritional fix.

While nobody would deny the value of research and management related to fat, sugar, and calories in our diet, excessive focus on nutrition can take away from the healing qualities and sheer enjoyment of eating, particularly eating with others.

This spiritual potential of food encompasses everything from the soil that produces what we eat, to the thoughtful act

---

[3] Kesten, 55–120.

of preparing and serving meals. Food, in the most profound way, brings us into community with others to listen, smell, and taste. Food tends to encourage intimacy and foster feelings of safety and well-being. Food also sparks memories and invites storytelling.

All of this probably explains why my mother always kept a food journal. Nowhere in its pages could we find any notations about how many calories or grams of sugar, fat, or protein were in her graham cracker cake or her crown roast of pork. On the other hand, she filled every line with lists of friends who came for dinner. She included the size of the turkey or roast beef she served, noted what people wore to her New Year's Eve supper, and jotted recipes for curried cheddar cheese ball appetizers and open-face sandwiches she served at my birthday parties. She noted snippets of cooking instructions, commented on her favorite dishes, made timetables, and listed birthday cake requests. Food, for her, delivered more than fuel to her guests. She understood the power of preparing and sharing good food, and she used it in a most hospitable way.

This food diary came to mind some time ago when my employer sold his publishing business to a large corporation. The new owner unceremoniously dismissed all the employees and closed our office. Ten of us lost our jobs. While the shock of unemployment created hardship for the entire staff, four of us agreed that whatever happened next, we would not permit this upheaval to bring an end to our friendship. Instead, we planned to convene frequently over food—food prepared by each of us; food that we would enjoy together for the next thirty years.

This proved to be a bigger commitment than we anticipated. Within a year, we all had taken separate paths. I moved to Saint Paul to continue my education. My friend Jackie exchanged city living for a large farm in rural Wisconsin. Kay found herself raising two grandchildren while her teenage daughter finished school, and Marcie accepted a job that kept her on the road or on a plane. Each of our families experienced the usual array of joyful achievements and celebrations, punctuated by plenty of upsets and do-overs.

The ensuing years have included new babies, graduations, and exciting professional accomplishments. Divorce, troubled children, alcoholism, and suicide also touched our lives. Yet one constant has remained: We come together with food as the common denominator. We laugh, cry, and encourage one another, while tackling everything from holiday krumkake to the Barefoot Contessa's beef bourguignon served with a good Cabernet. Though the four of us might not be the best cooks in the kitchen, we're always willing to give the KitchenAid mixer a chance. Sometimes it's perfection; other times someone forgets to add the flour. It really doesn't matter. What does matter is that the food and the time we spend preparing and sharing it is the glue that seals our shared life experiences and gets us on to the next chapter.

Andrew, the young man who came home from his misadventure, also benefited from the healing qualities of food. Whether he immediately recognized it or not, he soon began to see that so much of life was interconnected through the process of food preparation. The connection exists through the soil and rain, the workers who cultivate and harvest food, and the cook who prepares it. All are joined in a most profound and potentially healing way.

He also started to grow from the familiar routines surrounding food. He started to appreciate the predictability of sitting down with others and the safety and comfort of familiar rituals. As his energy increased, so did his hope. Eating with others who cared about him became a point of brightness. Slowly, over the course of time, he reacquainted himself with the textures and flavors of food and with the community of caring others who wished him good health. His halting homecoming became a cause for celebration.

Usually, when we talk about celebration, we mean festive events such as holidays, reunions, and anniversaries. We remember times when we have been able to forget the burdens of life and immerse ourselves in an atmosphere of music and merriment for a while. But celebration of the type Andrew and his family experienced means more than a party. This kind of celebration occurs only when fear and love, joy and sorrow can coexist without overwhelming us. Hence, to break bread with another is to celebrate by sharing the sustaining energy and power of life.

Consider This: Nothing Like the Perfect Dessert

Get out the mixer and whip up this fabulous cake from my grandmother Ida May for you or someone you love!

Andrew's Favorite Party Cake

2 cups sugar
1 cup unsalted butter, softened
3 large eggs
1 cup finely crushed graham cracker crumbs
1 cup whole milk
1¾ cups flour
2 tsp. baking powder
1 cup chopped walnuts
1 cup shredded coconut
2 tsp. vanilla

Cream butter and sugar until light. Add eggs one at a time, mixing between additions. Add vanilla. Roll graham crackers until fine and place in small bowl. Stir the milk into crumbs. Sift baking powder and flour together. Alternate adding graham cracker crumb mixture and flour, and mix until well combined. Stir in chopped walnuts and shredded coconut. Grease and flour two 9-inch round pans. Bake at 350 degrees for 30–35 minutes or until inserted toothpick comes out clean. Cool for five minutes and carefully unmold. Cool completely.

Filling
3 slices fresh pineapple, cut into cubes
2 bananas sliced

½ pint raspberries
1½ pint heavy cream, whipped and slightly sweetened

When cake is cool, place on large plate. Spread each layer with raspberry preserves. Layer mixed fruit on first cake and cover fruit with whipped cream. Place second cake on top of first and repeat process, covering the entire cake in whipped cream. Decorate with berries or fruit of choice, and serve.

12

Noah's Notes—Try On New Perspectives

When Madam and I got our Easter-dinner food assignment this year, we were surprised to find that it came with instructions. I had already selected my baking recipes, and she was all set to prepare a twelve-pound Nueske ham with sassy sweet-potato casserole. Then she read me the instructions on a Post-it Note, advising that we had better not tamper with tried-and-true holiday favorites. Our Minnesota nice host politely directed us not to show up with a pumpkin prune stollen or herbed yams with roasted artichokes. Apparently, she preferred not to rock the Easter bunny with any unorthodox flavors or newfangled potatoes.

The Post-it Note instructions prompted a déjà vu moment for me. A few years ago something similar happened when Madam's mother, Irene, suggested that the family celebrate Christmas on Christmas Eve. In previous years, they opened gifts and enjoyed their traditional meal on Christmas Day. If I'm not mistaken, Irene also tinkered with the menu that year. She substituted jellied cranberry sauce for the whole berry version. She also served the *rogue* cranberry sauce in a new glass bowl, rather than the one Grandma Ida May had given her years ago. She might have added nuts to the stuffing and a splash of almond extract to the whipped cream. In addition to these heretical menu violations, Irene had the nerve to move the Christmas tree to a different spot. Nobody even noticed that this move made it easier, not to mention safer, for everyone to enjoy a fireplace fire. According to Madam, Irene's reckless choices sent the entire family into a fit of apoplexy.

To say that Irene's attempts to refresh some tired old recipes and holiday decorations went smoothly would be a stretch. As evidence of her transgression, Madam's family members continue to retell the story about the year Irene ruined Christmas. A kind and generous woman who always sent me boxes of Harry & David colossal carrots every Christmas, Irene dared to fiddle with the familiar. Nobody let her forget it.

This set me to thinking about traditions. I once enjoyed a favorite tradition of demolishing my turnout blankets. These are the cozy rugs that horses wear when the weather gets nippy. Then I moved to Minnesota. One cold winter sporting nothing but my skivvies made a blanket believer out of me. Then there was the issue of horse trailers. I used to think those conveyances were made for cattle and companion goats. That was until I missed my book-signing party at the Saint Paul Saints baseball game, due to my resistance to stepping into a silly equine RV. Since that missed opportunity, my Comfy Sundowner trailer has become the centerpiece of our daily escapades.

It's safe to say that change, especially the kind of change that messes with our favorite traditions or modifies the way we've always thought about certain stuff, troubles most of us. Change can be as simple as adjusting our diets to correct an annoying muffin-top or as complex as Texas Hold'em poker rules. Change has pointed me in an entirely different direction, from the glamour of the racetrack to a new calling as an author and life coach for a Jack Russell terrier. Madam would also say that I've learned to make new and improved choices in girlfriends.

Anyhoo, since we got the Post-it Note Easter menu directives, Madam has been pontificating about change. It threatens to destroy the armor that protects our security, she claims, though I'm not so sure about that. She also says it sends up red flags of discomfort and leaves us feeling faintly unsettled or, in some cases, paralyzed. She must be referring to herself, because I don't recall feeling paralyzed, except when I first met one of those earlier girlfriends I mentioned.

So even though Madam's dissertation about change seemed slightly melodramatic, I must remember that she comes from a tradition of sermons. Come to think of it, she might consider amending that little custom to something less dictatorial.

In any case, I'll admit that an unexpected course revision pointed me toward many charming travel opportunities, funnier friends, and a lot more gin rummy. I've become a textbook example that proves even a horse can adapt. I'm a new man, wearing a snappy wool cooler and touring the Boundary Waters Canoe Area in my Comfy Sundowner trailer.

13

Concha Alborg—A Master of Adaptability

I don't think of myself as unbreakable. Perhaps I'm just
rather flexible and adaptable.
—Aung San Suu Kyi

Concha Alborg thought that nothing could hurt her more than the death of her husband. Then, just hours after his passing, she watched his death burst open a door to a more stunning loss. Her life as a widow had hardly begun when Concha learned that her marriage and her husband, Peter, were something other than what she had believed all those years. Perhaps it was her inherent gift of adaptability or her self-deprecating humor that helped Concha reconstruct her interrupted life. In any case, her story is one of reinventing self. It's a tale of a remarkable mother, wife, and grandmother entering a new chapter as a grounded and flourishing single woman.

Concha's Plan B began after twenty-one years of what she understood was a full and happy marriage. Her husband Peter, a guitarist and professor of music, died from esophageal cancer. During the three years from his diagnosis to his death, Concha and her daughters provided Peter with tender care, including home hospice. Very shortly after his death, Concha inadvertently learned that he had led another life, light-years away from their trusted partnership. It was her daughter who made this startling discovery while sorting through her stepfather's papers and personal effects. She found evidence in his computer of many intimate relationships outside his marriage. She further learned that his extracurricular activities began near the beginning of her mother's marriage to him and continued through her stepfather's illness.

"Needless to say, I was devastated," said Concha.

Irate might be a more accurate descriptor. Instead of grieving his death, she found herself grieving the loss of her innocence, of her marriage, of the life she had loved.

Born and raised in Spain during the troubling years after the Spanish Civil War and influenced by her academic father, Concha became a serious reader and student at an early age. She dreamed of becoming a writer. Then, just before her senior year in high school, she left Madrid and moved with her family to the United States. It was a move that ultimately defined who she is today—an immigrant living and writing between two cultures.

"Adaptability has always been my saving grace," she said. "Everyone thought it was terrible for my parents to uproot my brother and me and bring us to another country at such a tender age. Truthfully, I had a ball."

Instead of Franco's Spain, where young women faced suffocating repression, she felt an enormous amount of freedom in America. She delighted in after-school activities and opportunities that would not have been available to her in Spain. What could have been a difficult adjustment for a teenage girl in a new country opened doors for Concha. She found herself in an exciting new world where she earned her undergraduate degree, master's degree, and PhD in contemporary Spanish literature. From that point forward, whether she tackled a new language, culture, or country, Concha loved the adventure. Today, she enjoys visiting her family in Spain, though she never went back there to live.

Adaptable or not, after Peter's death Concha found herself mining all her best assets—and then some. One of her greatest frustrations was that she couldn't confront him to try to find out why he had deceived her. How had she not known or suspected something? Why did he leave evidence of his liaisons on his home computer, even throughout his time in hospice care? Was she living in denial for all those years?

Not at all, she thought. True, Peter traveled extensively, though he remained loving, kind, and seemingly engaged in their relationship, right up to the end. Concha felt so confident in their marriage that she and their daughters never suspected a thing. But everything changed at the end.

"I've always thought it was important to seek help when life gets tipped over," Concha said. "After Peter's death, my therapist suggested that I write him a letter, letting him know how I felt. The moment I saw myself on the written page, I began to heal. I could distance myself from the situation by writing. I could see myself as a character in a book. In this letter I told him that I was divorcing him." Thus, Concha found herself drawing upon another skill for surviving an interrupted life—her capacity to write a book, aptly titled *Divorce after Death. A Widow's Memoir.*

Once she started writing, Concha started to feel a sense of liberation from her grief. Even humor began to find its way into the gloom of loss and betrayal. Yet her biggest surprise came when she found forgiveness. "I had not thought about forgiveness when this happened or even while I was writing this book," she admitted. But then came a pivotal journey to the Middle East.

"Peter was Jewish, and I'm Episcopalian. He never wanted to go to Israel, though, and I found myself traveling to Israel and Jordan after his death."

Near the end of her pilgrimage, she also found herself in Jerusalem, standing at the Wailing Wall with her travel companions. They each placed notes in the wall. She felt compelled to write a note, forgiving Peter and telling him that he was free—and so was she.

Concha's trip to Israel also revealed to her that Peter's choices and the events that followed comprised only a single event in her history. What happened to her marriage has happened to countless others. Even closely held secrets have a way of finding the light of day. Whether immersed in life's high points or struggling with the low lights, a single event has not defined Concha's character or her capacity to heal and grow.

"The humor piece has been so helpful," said Concha.

She takes her work seriously, and there is nothing funny about lies and shattered families. Her painful exterior journey has evolved into an interior encounter with soul. Yet she has also had time to reflect on some amusing cameos in her story. For instance, near the end of Peter's life, when he was wrapping up his affairs (perhaps literally and figuratively), he asked that his body be sent to Johns Hopkins University for research purposes. While this was not an uncommon request, their home was not very accessible to motor vehicles.

"Where I live, it's not easy to make deliveries," Concha explained, "but they managed to come and pick up the body. Sometime later, I received a note from the postal service, saying that I had a package to pick up at the post office. Rather than drive, I decided to walk to pick up the package, which turned out to be his ashes. So I walked home carrying Peter's ashes under my arm while conversing with him along the way. It was Valentine's Day."

Her walk took place on the first romantic holiday after Peter's passing. She couldn't resist. With a captured audience under her arm and mischief on her mind, Concha launched what must have been an illuminating dissertation on celebrating Valentine's Day date with your cheating man.

Consider This: The Power of Telling Your Story

"The people who come to see us bring us their stories," says psychiatrist and writer Robert Coles. "They hope they tell them well enough so that we understand the truth of their lives."[4]

---

[4] Robert Coles, *The Call of Stories*, Houghton Mifflin, Boston, 1990. Pp. 7-9.

Anytime we invite someone to share a life story we are saying that she is valuable and her history is important. Since the story that grows from our past also contributes to the shape of the present and future, telling it is a valuable exercise. A life review also provides a solid platform from which to unpack a betrayal such as the kind Concha experienced. Writing, having conversations with friends, and examining family photos and letters can help one assimilate and integrate all kinds of setbacks that must be addressed before saying good-bye and moving on.

Consider a time when you felt duped or betrayed by a friend, partner or business associate. Describe how this development made you feel.

- Angry
- Hurt
- Humiliated
- Naïve
- Foolish
- Worthless

Articulating this kind of story involves caring for one's soul. It consists of a conversation that explores the meaning and value of our lives while helping us focus on closure.

14

Cultivate the Gift of Gratitude

For all that has been, thanks. For all that will be, yes!
—Dag Hammarskjold

My mother died in late July. I remember it as the season when fireweed and Queen Anne's lace bloomed along the roadsides near our Wisconsin home. Our father had passed five years earlier, though Mom, Mary Elizabeth Cook, remained in our family home, thanks to the tender care of a local farm woman named Mary Kapfer. Mom's death signaled the end of a chapter that defined our childhood and beyond. The essential center and gathering place we called home for all those years now stood empty, leaving my brother and me to tend to all the personal effects and financial affairs left behind. I remember saying to my brother, "We have become orphans." He agreed.

Far from a unique experience, the passing of parents touches us all, one way or another. Whether family relationships have enjoyed a history of warmth and support or bitter estrangement, the loss of parents marks a transition to something new. In this case, the something new would feature the end of memory making with my mother and a life without the safety net I once called home. Yet her passing also ignited in me an overwhelming feeling of gratitude that continues to greet me every day since her passing.

Shortly after my mother's death, a college roommate of mine from the sixties wrote to me, sharing her feelings upon the death of her second parent. Sarah grew up on a dairy farm near us, and I spent many childhood hours with her, galloping our ponies through the pastures and training her 4-H calves to put up with a halter and lead rope. She now lived in Ohio, and we had not seen one another since our last high school reunion.

Sarah wrote:

> The most distressing part for me was the fact that my father's death set off an inescapable chain of events. First, there was the process of sorting through a house indelibly marked by my parents' pastimes and business records—plaid flannel shirts worn thin from Dad's years of predawn barn chores; canceled checks written to the Menomonie Co-Op Equity. A dog-eared address book contained every one of my telephone numbers since college graduation. A calendar featured a color photo of their local bank. Something in the depth of me trembled with loneliness as I worked my way through everything from a grease-stained apple dumpling recipe to church directory photos of our neighbors, the Bauers. Inside a couple of hours I had taken a tour of their entire life on the farm, a slice of my history that now needed to be put to rest. There I sat, reviewing the plain threads and simple stitches that basted together the whole of my parents' marriage. I was at once moved by and envious of their uncomplicated life together. Their partnership spoke of a simplicity I had left behind years before. Never have I felt so alone and small.

> My sisters and I then held the classic farm auction to disperse of my father's treasured tools and machinery ... a small herd of Holstein heifers he kept when he stopped milking, an old Ford tractor, a combine, and several tons of hay.

Finally, we had to let go of our family farm property. We said good-bye to our cherished home, which had been a safe haven of predictability that welcomed us back whenever the world felt too noisy or complicated. I felt as if I had been cut loose from my moorings. Set adrift. Even strangely free. While I could accept the fact that my future would be appreciably different without my parents, I sensed that everything was now headed down an uncharted road, and I was supposed to be adult enough to direct the course. More frightening, I could already tell that this was a path I must make myself ... by walking it.

Sarah's story resonated with me on many levels. My mother's death had struck so many complex emotional chords, I hardly knew where to begin. Maybe I was just searching for clues to my own past and future. Or maybe the process of telling a story about a loved one could help set me off on the next leg of my journey. So I sat down to write the letter that I would send back to Sarah.

Dear Sarah,

My mother once gave me the entire collection of A. A. Milne's *Winnie-the-Pooh*. We both loved the books and often wrote down quotes from the characters and taped them to the refrigerator door. One quote came to mind today:

"Piglet noticed that even though he had a Very Small Heart, it could hold a rather large amount of Gratitude." ...

This short statement spoke volumes about my mother.

Her life and death bore much evidence of holiness, as in the Scottish word hale, or health, happiness, and wholeness.

Beyond her unconditional support of my brother and me and her companionable nature, she grasped a real understanding of good living. She lived this through her music, her friendships, and even in the comical ways that inspired her discipline of us children. She confirmed it daily through unpretentious fun— picnics on the bank of Elk Creek or midnight stargazing in the backyard. She was obsessed with Greek history. Loved to travel, seldom lost a gin rummy game, and could fly-fish her way to a boatful of walleyes. And we weren't the only ones who thought she was a keeper. Her friends called her an icon of hospitality and purveyor of good food. I never remember not wanting to see my mother.

Before she became frail and unable to drive, she loved touring through the countryside, tracking down morel mushrooms and purple vetch and teaching us how to identify them. With a bucket of water in the backseat and a *Peterson Bird Guide* in the glove box, we set out along the Chippewa River through Durand, Eau Galle, Ellsworth, and Spring Valley, Wisconsin. All the while, she offered a running commentary on everything from sandhill crane migrations to monarch butterflies, beekeeping, and how to spot poison sumac. At least once during every drive, she reminded us that it was impossible to see anything worth seeing from inside the car.

Maybe I was just romanticizing, or maybe it was her instinctive ability to look beyond the obvious for beauty. All I knew was, whenever we scrambled out of the car for one of her enforced nature walks, we witnessed a fascinating world that my brother and I still hold close. And, as she predicted, none of the roadside charm was visible from inside the car. My mother had a gift for raising up a common chipping sparrow to a place of reverence. She knew how to exalt the small stuff.

Years earlier, during the Great Depression when her family had very little money, she learned that to celebrate life together meant to appreciate its mix of hues and moods. Before "mindfulness" and being "in the moment" made it into the well-being lexicon, she knew all about being present to the daily experience of possibilities. She genuinely enjoyed the beauty of creation and the fundamental goodness of life. This explained why my daughter and a friend joined me on the day of my mother's funeral. We filled the car with buckets of water and took to the road to gather her favorite wildflowers for the church service.

As I wrote this to Sarah, I kept weighing whether or not this memory of my mother was an exaggeration or revision of our history. I concluded it was neither. Instead, writing this recollection reminded me of how often we construct mountains of obstacles, fortified by heaps of "should"s and "must"s that prevent us from being where our hearts want to be. How easy it is to get caught up in the battle for survival, the hectic and pressured tasks that define our days.

How easy it is to say, "If only I could do this, or find a better job, earn more money, or travel—then I could finally relax and begin to appreciate my life."

Actually, most of us probably don't need to change much in our lives to find an excuse to cheer. We really don't have to do big things, only small things well.

Shortly after writing this mini-memoir of my mother, I decided to honor that memory by going to her garden with a spade and a cardboard box. I eventually filled several boxes with her phlox and daylilies. I also found some nodding trillium she brought home from Lake Chetek and a jack-in-the-pulpit we sneaked into the car during one of our botanical hikes. I dug samples of everything that looked as if it could survive in my garden.

Next I called a few close friends to see if they had plants they would like to add to this new gardening enterprise. That produced several fancy specimens of iris, a white peony, and a shrub rose. Of course, all this plant life required more space, so I dug up as much of my yard as seemed sensible and fashioned new flower beds. Next, I labeled each plant, took photos with my smartphone as they bloomed, and produced a small sketchbook filled with pictures, sketches, and notes about each person who had given me a plant.

The garden became a living commentary on both family and friends. And right in the center lived my mother's wildflowers and famous "Resurrection" lilies that came from Oconomowoc and the garden of her best friend, Joan Horstick. The gardening enterprise took an entire summer to complete, but what a joy it has been ever since.

Today when I drive along the country roads of my childhood, I realize that a part of my mother still lives with my family in our garden. My Wisconsin home still greets us with rich fields of grain and verdant woodlands. Rural telephone lines host flocks of mourning doves that fly when we drive past. July is still the growing season of life in our hearts and in the soil of creation. It's still a time when the earth sends up new grass as it puts down deep roots.

July, for me, has become a spiritual moment and a doorway to the future, albeit a future changed by the passing of both my parents. But it's also a sign that I've turned the corner on another winter, slogged through a muddy spring, and plan to take a chance on a future of possibilities. July is a month when my thoughts always return to my garden, my childhood home, and my mother.

History and tradition do matter. For example, the Anglican tradition, in which I grew up, embraces a theology that highlights the earthly presence of God. Signs of this closeness brush our consciousness through magnificent cathedrals and other holy architecture. Music, poetry, stained glass, and gardens also fall within the promise of God's presence in the world. In its own way, each expression of beauty enhances our relationship with creation. In my experience, those who believe the world is inherently good, even though stained by pain and injustice, have a reason to say thank you.

Consider This: Caring for Myself and Others

Some people have a natural instinct for looking after their own well-being, especially at crossroads in their lives. They tend to reflect honestly on their places in time and then determine a healing course of action. Yet for many of us, and for those who watch and worry about friends and loved ones who don't seem to know how to take care of themselves, the following questions offer a place to begin.

Have I
- tended to my mental and emotional health?
- cared for my body and physical self?
- eaten well alone and with others?
- taken time to remember or say good-bye?

Am I
- nourishing my spiritual self?
- minding my important relationships?
- having some fun?
- attending to my creative self?
- beginning to think about the future?

15

Bruce Ferber—Kiss Your Creative Skills Hello

Every person harbors within himself or herself the artist's vocation to create, whether that is expressed in one's love for cooking or sewing, for dancing or loving, for storytelling or mechanical repairing. To encourage the artist in another is to create a spirit-filled community
—Matthew Fox, *On Becoming a Musical, Mystical Bear*

So many facets comprise healing and health. We typically think first of medicine and all the ways it can cure and mend the body and mind. Yet there are countless other elements that contribute to healing. Creativity, freedom, joy, connection to others, faith, and humor—all these and more enhance the quality of our lives and health. Such is the case of Bruce Ferber. An Emmy- and Golden Globe-nominated writer known for his inestimable contributions to popular television shows, Bruce's life and that of his wife, Jenise, and children, Aaron and Sarah, took a harsh turn when Jenise learned she had stage-three breast cancer.

Until this pivotal point in their lives, Bruce had enjoyed a twenty-year Hollywood comedy-writing career. Beginning as a lowly freelancer shopping a script for *Mash*, he went on to find success as a writer and executive producer for TV's popular *Home Improvement* and won a People's Choice Award.

His interest in comedy came to light early. "I was good at making people laugh," said Bruce. "This helped me enormously, since I was the shortest boy in the class." It also helped enormously when he started writing for television. Once he made it to Hollywood, the land of comedy and sitcoms, he found that a career in laughter was addictive.

"The thrill of seeing someone like Tim Allen get laughs from material I wrote was exciting," he added.

He also learned that one must do what he has to do to make it as a Hollywood television writer. This included eighty-hour workweeks laced with lousy carry-out food and long nights away from home. While he enjoyed working with other writers, the demanding schedules didn't guarantee success, often producing shows that got canceled, leaving the writers to scurry off in search of something new.

"The sitcom process is a group process," Bruce explained. "You want to be a team player, yet it has a way of muddying your own work. Plus, when you immerse yourself in all those hours working together, you lose contact with real people, including your family."

Jenise's diagnosis served as the catalyst for change in their lives. Though others encouraged Bruce to keep working, he found it increasingly tough to pitch sitcom pilots to twenty-five-year-olds, while his wife underwent chemotherapy. Contributing to television network meetings felt equally out of sync with activities going on at home. He eventually walked away and went home to be with Jenise and their children.

She was not well when he later met with Warner Bros. executives. Life was already shifting dramatically at home. The seriousness of Jenise's condition juxtaposed with the nonsense of the meetings made it clear to Bruce that he couldn't justify keeping this up.

Jenise died in 2006, leaving Bruce with a question: if his Plan A didn't fit anymore, how would he make a Plan B? Unquestionably, his young children needed extra care and attention. He also had to discern what he needed to help keep him moving forward. In addition to becoming a single parent, he now had to confront the task of rebuilding his own personal and professional life.

He knew he had to leave the world of Hollywood sitcom writing but didn't know where to go or what to do. "I'd sit in the meetings, and my eyes would glaze over," Bruce admitted. "The sitcoms seemed foolish in the face of our family's loss."

Yet he couldn't sit around bemoaning his fate when he had children that kept him focused on their future together. "I had to regroup and ask myself, 'Who am I? If I'm going to continue writing, what makes me think I have anything to say?'

"Some people have regrets and get stuck with each change of direction or loss that life hands them," he offered. "It's not uncommon for many of us to look at what we've done wrong, to feel guilt, and to ruminate." Then there are others who keep progressing and growing with relative ease, even when faced with a rough transition.

"I'm fascinated with people's second acts," he added. "When you work in the entertainment business, you want to get out before they show you the door. It's an ageist business, and the exit age is about forty."

He was about to meet his own second act. A quintessential writer, Bruce began to see an opportunity for the talented, persistent, and creative part of him to take a chance on something new. Something better. He had already put in the hard work and now would take the leap and show what he was all about.

"I always liked writing prose, and I kind of challenged myself to see whether I could pull off a novel," he said. "I wanted to write something deeper and more personal that explored a range of emotions you can't deal with in sitcoms."

So he did it. He wrote his first book, *Elevating Overman*, published in 2012. He enjoyed the experiment from beginning to end. It became a grand adventure, as well as a way to grow and heal. He was approaching life differently this time. A fundamentally shy guy, he found himself getting out of his comfort zone and speaking in front of crowds. He had to go out and promote the book, and he surprised himself by meeting many wonderful people along the way.

"The book is about a character searching for meaning and gets a second chance," Bruce explained. "After Jenise's passing, I too was offered a second chance. The character Overman wondered why good things were happening to him. Meanwhile, I was having similar experiences. This Ira Overman was giving me my second chance."

Bruce determined that this fictional caper also helped him become a better father and marked the beginning of a whole new set of life experiences. It turned out to be a fantastic adventure that continues to evolve.

The guy simply loves to write. When describing his new life as a novelist, he noted author Stephen King's response when someone asked him why he wrote such creepy stuff. His answer, "What makes you think I have a choice?" Today, Bruce might offer a similar, albeit humorous, take on himself: "I'm not a stand-up comic. I remain a writer committed to a life of quiet masochism."

Bruce sustained a hard midstream reversal, one that highlights the subject of fairness. Why isn't life fair? If we choose to believe in God or a higher power, we must convince ourselves of a loving God. Yet how do we make sense of a loving God who would take a child or dish out unspeakable pain to good people? When we ask, "Why? What's the meaning of this?" we are asking questions that are essential to being human. They are also essential to becoming whole again.

"We need time to absorb the magnitude of the bad stuff and not just brush it away or deny it," said Bruce. "I'm eight years down the line from Jenise's passing, and I still think it's unfair. She won't see her daughter get married or her grandchildren grow up. I'll always see it as unfair, though I must and I will keep walking the path."

The idea of getting over it isn't helpful. In my experience, loss is not about handling things well or keeping it all together. It's more about keeping afloat in a rising tide of doubt. Asking the silence "why" is how we find our way to coexisting with an uninvited visitor. Healing happens where fear and love, joy and sorrow, tears and smiles can forge a lasting peace.

When anxiety wakes Bruce at night, he struggles through, tries to get to sleep, and comes to resolution in the morning. "Always wait until morning to deal with difficult subjects," he adds. Wise advice.

Each day sheds new light on his new walk. Bruce followed his passion, completely leaving his show business past behind. Now, surprisingly, his past has come back to visit him. On a whim, he sent the book to former colleague and fellow comic Jason Alexander to see if he liked it; he did. So Bruce invited Jason to record the audio book. Not only did Jason accept the invitation, but he also arrived at the studio with a different voice for every male and female character. Hearing the audio book inspired Bruce to write a script.

"It made me laugh so much, I went to work on the screenplay," said Bruce.

Though he never wrote the book with the intention of its becoming a movie, the prospect became more intriguing when capable producers took an interest. The adventure continues.

A review of *Elevating Overman* sums up Bruce's journey and the creative gift that has propelled him from a derailed life plan to a captivating new expedition. It reads:

Elevating Overman is about a middle-aged Jewish guy who gets a second chance in life. It is what he does with this second chance the "elevates" Overman. Now, unlike Ira Overman, I am a Gentile. But like Ira Overman, I was given the gift of a second chance to elevate me. My second chance in life gave me the opportunity to befriend the author. Bruce Ferber, who was our head writer on *Home Improvement*, and albeit a short man, is a very clever, insightful, and funny fellow indeed. That alone gives me the confidence to say, "Congratulations Bruce—you've done it again."

—Tim Allen, actor, author, and comic

Consider This

Recovering from an event or illness that knocks a person off the rails requires time, patience, and a gentle hand—one's own gentle hand. An honest self-examination can heighten spirits, provide new direction, and enhance one's sense of well-being.

- When was the last time you forgave yourself? Forgave another?
- List ten things that nurture your spirit. When did you last practice these?
- What causes you to lose energy?
- How can you detach from these to protect yourself from energy drain?
- Do you have important relationships that need healing? If so, how do you plan to attend to these?

16

Trust the Power of Plain and Small Things

In character, in manner, in style, in all things, the supreme
excellence is simplicity.
—Henry Wadsworth Longfellow

You could call it nature's last hurrah for the year. Certainly October, with its bright skies and brilliant color, provides one of my native Wisconsin's finer selling points. Yet along with its beauty, a sense of the tragic surrounds this mysterious month. The leaves reach the height of glory just before they fall to the ground to die. The earth, having given up its harvest, suddenly turns inward to rest and recharge. In October, we see the coming and going of active life.

For me, October also raises questions about human potential and human limitations—all those questions that follow us through our important life transitions. On one hand, it washes the countryside with exquisite pigments. On the other hand, it reminds us that we will soon face winter and its snowy hardships. So one might say that October exposes the fragile nature of all life, including human life. This is the month of Halloween, or Samhain, a Celtic word meaning summer's end. According to ancient tradition, this celebration of Samhain marked the beginning of the season of hope and of memory, when the gods came and walked upon the earth for a while. And according to pre-Christian religious traditions in Britain and Ireland, October marked the beginning of the sacred season during which the earth and her inhabitants retreated to their roots to be rejuvenated.

October is a perfect time to look beyond the brief cycles of nature and her killing frosts toward truths that hold up through the years. The October mystery encourages us to ask ourselves, "How do we choose to lead our lives? How do we maintain confidence in a world infused with both frightening disorder and brilliant possibilities? How do we live fully and well, wherever we happen to find ourselves? Where can we turn for sustenance and courage?"

Jewish theologian Abraham Heschel said that the spiritual life is a matter not of acquiring information but of learning to see the world in a new way. Sometimes this new way of seeing means discovering a new path, or learning to coexist peacefully when an old one is gone or no longer viable. Other times it might be a matter of learning to see the world in an old way. American culture, with its penchant for measuring and managing numbers and outcomes, does not fully appreciate this approach. Google Analytics simply doesn't provide a measurement for feeling, listening, and intuitively sensing the world's wisdom. How easy it has become to complicate our lives with "content-driven busyness." Technology wires us to work and fuels us to the point of exhaustion. Perhaps one of life's biggest challenges today is keeping it simple.

Working for years with sick children and those who care for them has taught me that keeping it simple means everything to the people I meet. Their lives have already become hugely complicated. Rarely do chaplains get to visit or play with well children. Beyond a game of Bingo or an occasional hospital visit from sports celebrities, we mostly find parents exhausted, keeping vigil in a surgery waiting room, critical care unit, or a newborn intensive care nursery. In these settings, families must give away much of their power. Like it or not, they have to let go of the selves that can supervise things, organize things, and control things. Even things as simple as walking a child to the school bus or managing personal privacy feel out of reach. While hospital caregivers march confidently through their medical task lists, families find themselves having to trust and wait. Parents feel exceedingly vulnerable and often bond with other families in similar circumstances. As the minutes and hours pass, social barriers dissolve. Complete strangers cling together, held by a tender thread of hope, mixed with a large dose of apprehension. All the familiar markers of yesterday's plans fall into disarray.

Most of us experience hospitals as places where complicated, even heroic acts take place, especially a hospital exclusively for children, where sophisticated technology can save the life of a baby born too early. Surgeons perform intricate heart procedures on down-covered infants small enough to fit neatly in the palm of an adult hand. Other medical specialists operate intricate ventilators that sustain the lives of tiny babies whose lungs have not yet developed. I have witnessed spectacular medical miracles at the hands of astute neonatologists and pediatric neurosurgeons.

In spite of these remarkable advances, I'm often captivated by how the extraordinary breaks into ordinary daily events. Feeding, bathing, housekeeping, teaching, consoling, and encouraging—these are the routine elements of care that take on new meaning for families who have been unceremoniously dropped into in this medical world. Far more than kind acts of concern, these plain and simple actions become powerful signs of continuity. Somehow basic tasks performed day by day and year by year generate a rhythmic, life-sustaining order that truly can be trusted. I view it as proof that the center still holds, even in the midst of chaos.

The Celtic approach to God opens up a world where nothing is too common to be exalted, and nothing is so exalted that it cannot be made common. Heaven lies "a foot and a half above the height of man," said an old woman from County Kerry in the southwest of Ireland. The Celts have provided the world with a wealth of prayers and poems from the frontiers of England, Wales, Scotland, and Ireland. Celtic spirituality, once almost forgotten, has enjoyed a strong revival. Its humble, homely approach to God was born out of harsh lives often spent in conditions of extreme poverty and relentless work.

The Celts were ordinary people who took the tasks of their daily lives and treated them sacramentally, as outward and visible signs of an inward and spiritual grace. Celtic spirituality took common things and interpreted them as signs of a greater reality. Getting up in the morning and carrying out one's duties of washing, making the fire, milking and weaving, fishing and farming all testified to a holy presence in creation. Nearly everything that happened between birth and death could become an occasion for recognizing the closeness of God.

Viewed in its entirety, the Celtic approach to spiritual life offers both reassurance and honesty, at times when other spiritual resources might not resonate. Too often the religious or spiritual messages we receive say that God's presence can only be confirmed in certain places or through prescribed events, by some revolutionary improvement or radical conversion. Likewise, secular human successes come only through the highest level of production and achievement. Rarely is anyone rewarded for being somewhere in the middle and certainly not for being plain or modest. The problem with this is that most of us don't find our days filled with news-making events, front-page deeds, or headline tributes.

It's easy to fall into the trap of believing that any hope of attaining the good life lies in our ability to earn our way in through perfect marriages or smooth-sailing careers. In fact, the world might feel more hospitable if we learned to simply live out each day in the knowledge that success is as close as our simple routines and small commitments. It's those shared, ordinary events and stale transactions that keep us grounded and well. They make up the loom on which we weave a strong and serviceable garment. This idea might be one of the most profound, though difficult, truths that we ever learn.

Each of us is ultimately called not to achieve or attain but to make her own path toward inner peace. We are invited to walk on the sacred ground of our human experience, the ordinary, unspectacular, and sometimes painful experience of our time together. Each day hands us new adventures and new paths toward completion. Each passing year and life-transition shines new light on the meaning of our days and the hope for our future.

Whether it's Celtic spirituality, familiar routines at work or the ease of hanging out with a good friend, I believe that the real power lies in the plain and simple aspects of celebrating life together. When I find myself feeling world-weary or without easy answers, I also find myself longing to be with those I love and simply enjoy the beauty of creation. Yet I suspect that most of us often let a mountain of obstacles prevent us from being where our hearts want to be. We get caught up in the battle for survival—the hectic, pressured, competitive, and exhausting experiences of the day. Ironically, the real gift that waits to be accepted at the end of the day is likely to be as humble as walking the dog.

The poet Robert Frost often wrote about the seasons. In his poem "November," he described the subtle beauty of late fall in much the same way as the season of Samhain. Frost's poem also captures the mood of that quiet interlude before winter. It sets the stage for a reflective time when we start to prepare for months of cold and ice. November, for those of us who live in the upper Midwest, is nature's introduction to an icy assault.

We are, in some ways, products of our earth's seasons. The fall calls us to reach into the depths of our lives, to examine our plans and perhaps redesign them. We move indoors and enter the interior recesses of our hearts. In both cases, the watchwords are "wait" and "listen." Wait for snow. Wait for cold. Listen for spring sounds. Wait for wisdom.

Meanwhile, we do our waiting in a world of *doing* and achieving. So we are wise to remember that in the fall, when the earth and her inhabitants settle into violet stillness, it might be a sign that life itself is waiting for us to slow down, simplify, and clear the way to important destinations.

Consider This: Sorting and Simplifying

The passing of seasons and life-transitions tends to open our eyes to the meaning and measure of our days. Some might call this the aging process. For me, the experience has been more like peeling an onion and removing the protective exterior to reveal the part that sparks up my next salad. Each new day has become a process of tidying my space and clarifying my priorities. Though this sorting and simplifying process might be associated with growing older, I believe it is vitally important to being whole and well at any age or stage in life.

Think about the role routines play in your life. Consider all those little habits and practices that you have developed over time. Do you find them tiny little annoyances or sources of energy and harmony?

Do they

- bring a sense of calm to your day?
- help you clarify your thoughts and plans?
- prepare you for work?
- create a feeling of continuity?
- influence your important relationships?

17

Fred Krehbiel—A Case of Resilience, Born of Kindness

Once you have made peace with the present moment, see what happens, what you can do or choose to do, or rather what life does through you. There are three words that convey the secret of the art of living, the secret of all success and happiness: One with Life. Being one with life is being one with Now. You then realize that you don't live your life, but life lives you. Life is the dancer and you are the dance.

—Eckhart Tolle

Fifty years ago, if someone had asked Fred Krehbiel about his Plan B, he probably would not have mentioned expanding the family electronic component business to Japan. Yet with a $25,000 budget—including his own salary—and a charge to grow the company called Molex overseas, he set out to capture the interest of Japanese customers in electrical connectors. This enterprising plan launched a chronicle of innovative business successes and distinctive personal investments that would define Fred as a resilient, kind, and savvy entrepreneur.

Fred's original career choice, or his Plan A, had little to do with electronics and everything to do with international travel and diplomacy. "I wanted to go into the diplomatic corps," he explained. "Once I finished college, I headed for Georgetown University to do graduate work in preparation for this."

An odd twist of fate squelched this plan when he realized his dyslexia, a relatively misunderstood condition in the 1960s, would create a significant challenge to his learning the two required foreign languages. It also would impede his taking graduate school tests.

"It became apparent to me at Georgetown that I wasn't going to pass this test or make it in the diplomatic corps," said Fred simply. "So the question was, 'Now what am I going to do?' Fortunately, at that age, if one thing didn't work out, something else would, so my transition from Plan A to Plan B wasn't that traumatic."

After serving a stint in the Air Force Reserve program, he sat down with his father to talk about a possible future at Molex. John Krehbiel suggested that since his son was interested in international travel, maybe he would like to start developing Molex across the globe. Hard to imagine, but at that time, when company executives got queries from overseas about Molex products, they just threw them away.

Fred accepted the challenge and started his new job with just enough money to pick one international market. While most American companies were expanding in Europe, he chose to begin in Japan. So what started with an interest in the world, followed by an inability to pass exams and learn foreign languages, turned into an opportunity to travel and appreciate the international aspects of growing a business.

"This opportunity would never have happened if I hadn't failed at the diplomatic corps," said Fred with a chuckle. "So Molex became my Plan B."

Fortuitously, Molex entered the Japanese electronics industry in 1970, a time of the industry's rapid growth. Fred encountered a country producing a tremendous number of electronic products, which eventually set the standard worldwide.

From that point forward, Molex's unconventional direction of expansion also featured a somewhat unconventional business model. It was based on "becoming local" and adjusting to the culture of the region in order to meet the needs of the local customer. Senior Molex executives were required to live in at least one other global market place around the world.

"You can't have an international company run by a bunch of Midwesterners," Fred explained. "We wanted to create an international team, an early goal that still stands. We believed we could work together more effectively if we had lived outside our comfort zones." Japan eventually became Molex's most profitable operation and served as a pivotal point in their business and Fred's career. A second plant opened in Ireland in 1971. Today, Molex operates fifty-eight factories in nineteen countries.

One needs only to pick up a copy of *Forbes* magazine or a *Wall Street Journal* to see the level of success Fred has experienced. Yet equally inspiring are the observations of his friends and associates about his kindness and innate generosity.

To know Fred is to appreciate his intrepid approach to life and the art of living. Call him a unique visionary, or maybe just a man who knows what counts and wastes little time on what doesn't. His can-do attitude colors everything and everyone around him. Those closest to him are convinced he inherited a set of ethical and personal priorities from his distant Mennonite kinfolk. These speak of values such intercultural competence, hospitality, and hard work.

His attention to others, even relative strangers, is legend. There was the Sherpa who assisted Fred during a 1981 hiking expedition in Tibet. Once the Sherpa, named Phurba, expressed interest in gaining employment in the United States, Fred went to work. He first hired Phurba to work for Molex, Ireland, where he stayed for four years. Next he found a position for Phurba in the Lisle, Illinois-based Molex, where he remains employed today. Phurba and his wife, Douma, have raised and educated two children in this country and continue to keep close contact with the Krehbiel family.

Or there was Fred's guide, Kibet, whom he met during a safari in Kenya. Kibet approached Fred about the prospect of getting his son, Kip, into college in the United States. After a good deal of footwork, Fred was able to secure enrollment for Kip at Benedictine College in nearby Lisle, Illinois. Upon his arrival, Kip faced more than a few cultural and cold-weather challenges, though he persevered and made it to the finish. He completed college and returned to Kenya, where he has applied his hard-earned cultural and academic skills in his home community.

Evidence of Fred's attentiveness to others' needs and interests shows up in unexpected places—with lifelong friends, among Molex employees, and even with long-lost relatives.

Take a distant cousin, Adele. As a child, Adele had been struck by an electric car and sustained a permanent neurological injury that for years kept her wheelchair-bound and out of the limelight. When Fred discovered her, she was up and able to care for herself, working as a medical records assistant for the University of Chicago—a job she enjoyed for over forty years. She kept a modest apartment and a pet cat named Smokey.

Fred learned about Adele sometime after college and decided he wanted to get to know her. So he found her phone number and rang her up. Once they became reacquainted, he started visiting Adele regularly. He could see that keeping an apartment posed a challenge for her and thought maybe she would appreciate a little help with maintenance and upkeep. She agreed, and help she got. Fresh paint, comfy furniture, and a crisp new "up-do" marked the beginning of a long and rewarding relationship with Adele.

The relationship grew and soon found Adele enjoying herself at Fred's parties and family gatherings. She even accompanied him and his Irish bride, Kay, on their honeymoon trip around the world. Photos of Adele touring and riding elephants started popping up in family photo albums. She flourished and so did all those who came to know her.

So what does it mean for someone like Fred to find himself surrounded by considerable wealth and the capacity to choose how to use it? For him, it has always meant options—

the option to shepherd an employee with a serious health threat through a level of health care diagnostics he could not otherwise have afforded; the option to attend to the well-being and interests of relatives and friends; the option to explore the world and its cultures and arts; the option to preserve and protect priceless antiquities; and of course, the option to support meaningful philanthropic organizations and charitable causes.

"Once you realize you have financial freedom, you have incredible options," said Fred. "It's how you use your wealth that matters. Where you take it is up to you. It isn't the money itself that is so striking but the opportunities you have to make a difference with it."

One place it has taken him and his wife, Kay, is deep into Irish art, architecture, and gardens. It began with the purchase of an eighteenth-century farmhouse, located in County Kerry, Ireland, within miles of Kay's large family. Once they completed the much-needed restorations, he and Kay realized they had nothing to hang on the walls. Thus began their quest to fill their historic home, Churchill House, with Irish art and more.

"We decided to try to tell the whole story of Irish art from the earliest days to today," said Fred. "I've always felt that art is wonderful, but it really resonates with people when shown in its context. We tried to put together a series of rooms that became home to eighteenth-century furniture, glass, and other objects of art."

The result was a remarkable collection showing the various periods of Irish art in context. Churchill House now consists of a stunning assortment of walled gardens, a thatched cottage, a library, stables, grottos, and a garden pavilion, to name just a few. Each has been restored or recreated into an eighteenth-century host of Fred and Kay's collection of Irish treasures. And Churchill House was just the beginning.

About ten years after the restoration of Churchill House, Fred eagerly took on another project, Ballyfin. Located at the foot of the Slieve Bloom Mountains in the Midlands center of

Ireland, the early nineteenth-century mansion offered a "pristine ruin" begging to be restored. Partnering with design consultant Jim Reynolds, Fred and an army of artisans, contractors, and interior designers set out to restore Ballyfin to elegance, including a memorable collection of Irish, English, and French art and antiquities. It took ten years, but even the original species of trees and vegetation have been replanted. The ancestral home of the British Coote family has now been transformed, detail by detail, into a small luxury hotel.

Time has passed, the Krehbiel family has sold Molex, and Fred has certainly reached a respectable retirement age. However, retirement is not a word that appears in his lexicon. Undaunted by stereotypes, at age seventy-four he has spearheaded a new business and continues to live life large. He prefers sea kayaking to Medicare moments and gently chides his contemporaries who've been attending downsizing seminars. He's already planned the next "friend group travel reunion." This year's annual event will convene in the Pacific Northwest and include a group of friends who have celebrated their time together for decades.

"Of course, there are health and real challenges that go with aging," added Fred. "When we plan a trip with friends, I tell them, if I get a good medical report, I'll be happy. And if I get a bad one, we'll go anyway."

Given that philosophy, it's not surprising that every month features global travel for Fred. It also includes time in Ireland to enjoy Churchill House, Ballyfin, and all the guests and family members that go with each.

"When you get older, you have to fight like crazy not to let your life get smaller and smaller," said Fred. "You retire from your job. You lose wonderful friends. You encounter health problems. This just means it's time to get out and find new things that interest you. Get busy and meet new people. Hang out with young people as much as you can, and be willing to get out of your space and extend yourself."

Many who know Fred Krehbiel would agree it's never been a matter of his saying yes or no to life. It's always been a matter of his living the life that wants to live in him—for as long as he can. Not only has he achieved this, but he's brightened the paths of countless others along the trail.

Consider This: Moving Forward with Resilience

Plans change, sometimes through our own doing and sometimes resulting from complications, adversity, or simply the evolution of time and circumstances. In each case, resilience, or accepting one's new reality, often can clear the way to new and exciting dreams.

Have there been times when, faced with what you considered a failure, you relied on your own resilience to move through an obstacle?

- Describe the process and the result of adapting to your new reality.
- Most of what we learn in life begins with a question or a problem. List some examples of questions or problems you have negotiated.
- Name a pivotal point when an unexpected change has brought you meaningful new insights and discoveries.

18

Noah's Notes—Time to Get Unstuck

If this writing life qualifies as my Plan B, it certainly has presented some pesky problems for a horse. Daily keyboard tasks have knocked the stuffing out of my leisure pursuits. All those memorable hours once filled with gin rummy and Hoofleball tournaments have been replaced with Google Analytics and search-engine-optimized tweeting drills. And here's another sticky wicket—writer's block. I suppose writer's block fits into the general *stuck* category, though it was something that caught me by surprise. It also has been preventing me from reaching my next goal—completion of a literary masterpiece!

Take social media. I know it's a must for bloggers and other aspiring aspirers. Whether pitching recipes for gluten-free cupcakes or kale soufflé, savvy cooks everywhere are online, chatting up their prospects. Frankly, I love to bake, though I find myself speechless when it comes to posting a "how-to" featuring ten quick methods for peeling a carrot.

Then there is the issue of my Wordpress website. When Madam told me it was my job to manage the "back door" of this thing, I thought she meant the back door—that place where Waconia Feed and Seed deposits my groceries. But no; I'm now busy uploading blog posts and trying to size photos smaller than a barn door. Actually, I'm *not* uploading blog posts because I'm stuck and unable to squeak one out.

Then there's the Facebook challenge. I'm never short of ideas, but getting the words in the "What have you been up to?" box feels like technical quicksand to a horse. That, plus my fans ask me bewildering questions. "Can I come to work for you?" queried a teenage girl from Oregon. "Will you marry me?" came from a divorcee in Cincinnati. "What musical instrument do you play?" asked a Bob Dylan fan from Duluth.

And finally, my friend Gabe, the cribbage whiz, offered to help set up my Twitter account. A retired equine law enforcement officer, Gabe now spends a lot of time online studying cribbage CliffsNotes. This explains his technical skills, as well as why he never loses a game. So given his love affair with his iPad, I assumed he knew something about Twitter. He did, or at least he knew enough to set up my account. He then shouted *Ciao* and departed for a Las Vegas poker tournament, leaving me to manage the fallout. And there was fallout.

My first Twitter follower called herself "Sweet Cheeks" and wanted to meet me under the Yum Yum tree. Geez, that was a new one. The next arrival claimed to be "Anything Goes." This one included an impressive selfie as evidence that anything and everything resembling clothing had already gone. This alerted me to change my profile from tall, dark, and handsome fellow to tall, dark, and handsome gelding. It helped, though the whole experience left me with keyboard paralysis.

Anyhoo, Madam cautioned me about writer's block when I signed on to pen a first book with her. Since she tends to exaggerate, I just smiled amiably and ignored her warning. This has not deterred her from continuing to offer tips on writer's block.

"Noah, all it takes is a simple thank-you note to your mother-in-law, or a term paper on downy woodpeckers to set off writer's block," she declared. "One minute you whip out a pen and prepare to dazzle your readers, and the next minute you hit the editorial cellar." She spoke like a woman with some experience at this, though I don't have a mother-in-law, so I quickly dismissed her example.

She then explained that symptoms vary, though always include avoidance tactics. The condition can come on abruptly, as an overpowering urge to get a tattoo instead of sending a birthday card to your brother. Or it can strike cunningly, leaving its victim powerless to write anything more than today's date. The avoidance tactics resonated somewhat with my experience.

"So what does this writer's block look like?" I queried with casual interest. "Does it cause hives, or grow like mildew on a budding novelist's forehead? I have a friend who might want to know." I chuckled.

Madam ignored the mold analogy and pressed on with her examples.

"Writer's block has caused me to feel overcome with a sudden yearning to schedule a colonoscopy," she offered. "One time I found myself inexplicably enrolled in an auto mechanics class, just to avoid writing a press release. And there was the day last fall when I stayed home for the weekend to make clothes for the cat," she said with a sigh. Each of these occasions led to a nap, followed by supper and an itch to take a quick spin through the house with the Hoover upright."

Good grief, this sounded bad. It also sounded familiar. Just yesterday, Gabe mentioned that I looked plump, and my turnout blanket hugged me like a new pair of Spanx Shapewear. All this time I thought it had shrunk in the dryer. True, I've been busy in the kitchen, testing my apple pan dowdy recipes. And I wonder how many Louis L'Amour gunslinger novels I've finished this month.

So I asked Madam, "Hypothetically, what would you suggest for a gifted author who might possibly be stuck in a writer's block snag?"

"Well," she offered with a faint smile, "whoever that writer is, he could begin to get his groove back by writing an apology note to his landlord for making a wholesale mess of the party room."

"Hmm … it's certainly is worth a try," I replied. "I'll also be sure to share this information with Gabe. He'll find it helpful."

"Indeed," said Madam.

19

When a Plan Must End

I have finally begun to see the difference between giving up,
giving in,
and knowing when I've had enough.
—Author unknown

A colleague of mine named Jill shared a story of her long ordeal with ulcerative colitis. This chronic inflammatory condition, characterized by tiny ulcers and small abscesses throughout the lining of the colon, had nearly destroyed her health. Not only had she lost a significant amount of weight since we last met, but she could hardly eat even a small meal without suffering pain and an urgent need to rush to the bathroom. Yet Jill pressed on with her responsibilities, including two jobs, plus caring for her aging parents and an active toddler. Listening to her talk, I was struck by how easily she had slipped into a pattern of impossible demands and unrealistic expectations of herself. Her dilemma posed a question: how does one recognize and redirect such a winless situation before sacrificing one's health and well-being?

Jill had done her homework well—at least homework regarding her medical condition. She dug into an exhaustive literature and online search, visited several competent medical specialists, and made the rounds at an internationally acclaimed medical center. Unhappy with the answers and treatments she received from all the experts, she expanded her search into the field of integrative therapies. She tried acupuncture and signed up with a naturopath. She made appointments with massage therapists, herbalists, and a traditional Chinese medicine practitioner. None offered her any relief. In fact, she became even more ill.

Finally, frustrated and angry with the entire medical establishment, Jill made an appointment at a local healing center whose comprehensive approach to treating illness included a variety of alternative therapies. Her first visit was supposed to include a thorough health history, followed by a consultation with an internal medicine physician who would coordinate her care. But by this time, Jill had little interest in holistic approaches to health. She was, in her words, tired of wasting precious time. As might be expected, the visit got off to a bad start and went further downhill when the center's dietitian recognized the need to involve other health professionals in Jill's diagnosis and treatment plan. Jill stormed out and demanded a refund for what she called a *wasted* appointment.

"I've done all that!" she exclaimed tearfully. "The last thing I need is for someone to take an inventory of the way I live. All I want is a diet that works."

Never during this whole process had Jill told her health practitioners that she was recently divorced. Nor did anybody learn about her struggles to balance childcare with her professional perfection and her impossible work schedule that demanded long road trips. Her complicated albeit *productive* life, framed by smartphones, webinars, and Skype conferences, was literally squeezing the guts out of her. Now she found herself demanding a cure for a complicated medical condition.

Jill's expectations of herself *and* the medical community seemed unrealistic, if not outright irrational. Yet the same could be said of society's expectations of Jill and countless others—against all odds, be productive! In fact, Jill never did seem to recognize the meaning of her body's persistent protests against her lifestyle. She also couldn't see a need to attend to the larger picture or her overall well-being. Lost somewhere in a maze of prescription drugs and diagnostic procedures was Jill's assessment of what this illness meant to her. And it meant a lot. Colitis had become her life. Besides causing her obvious physical pain, it left her feeling that she couldn't take care of herself anymore, much less the rest of her family. Her performance at work dropped, threatening her job security and causing even more anxiety. In her search for a cure, Jill had ventured far outside her medical insurance coverage and faced huge bills. Her losses included her health, money, clients, security, personal power, and autonomy. Jill's Plan A was not viable anymore, nor was her goal of getting well any time soon.

No single element of Jill's situation held the answer to her health dilemma, but it's safe to say that she and countless women and men lead depleting lives that defy health of body and spirit. And expecting her physician to simply "fix" the situation was not fair. Yet telling someone like Jill to simplify her life is not enough. She is the one who must ultimately discover what self-knowledge and simplicity could bring to the quality of her life.

If wisdom originates in simplicity, it also grows from simply daily events, from the plain encounters and unadorned stories that belong to each of us. These are the windows through which we can rediscover a sense of certainty and peace that inform the quality of our lives. They also provide the foundations on which we can build our own formula for living well, something to which Jill had never given an ounce of thought.

While I was growing up, nobody warned me that my life would be defined largely by my ability to take care of myself and my children on my own. Nor would I have guessed that corporate mergers and management upsets would bounce me from one career to another. I found myself divorced, returning to school, praying to hang on to a paycheck, protecting my children, and carving out a little time at the lake to recover from each week's pressure and responsibilities. It was not an easy time but a time when I started to see the world in which I grew up as a trustworthy guide for making future decisions.

This world ultimately changed the direction of my journey and continues to inform my long-term plans.

It began in a small Wisconsin town, a rural setting where hardwood hillsides and acres of corn shaped the spiritual center from which I still draw nourishment, due in large part to the mother I have already described. I still mine the essence of that time and place—not in hopes of returning to the "good old days" but with a kind of trust that says *yes* to the lessons of the earth that my brother and I learned many years ago.

Today, when I go home to visit during the harvest season, I again feel the truth and rhythm of this quieter world. It's still a place where, sometime late in August, summer stands still, as we all must at some point. That's when the growing pauses to reflect before turning homeward toward autumn. The breeze drops to a sultry stillness. A subtle shift of air stretches the clouds across the humid sky. The piercing whir of cicadas punctuates the air. Corn has tasseled and oats are gone from the fields. Round bales stand in orderly columns at the fence line. Grass along the roadside has gone to seed, and a few grapes hang from spindly vines. It is a scene that says another growing season is drifting quietly toward fruition. And now it's time to harvest the bounty.

This picture frames little more than an average summer day in a world that has little time for average. To be average is to fall short. Being average means not *doing*. Enough. A state of average veers dangerously close to failure. Being average doesn't pay especially well, either. Instead, we hear that success comes through accomplishing above-average feats. Success means doing rather than being. We are what we do. We are important when we do something important. We are intelligent if we do something intelligent. We are valuable when we do something valuable. We are powerful if we do something powerful or, perhaps, when we take someone else's power away. This world, Jill's world, speaks little of health or well-being.

The real eye-opener about this world is that most of us, like a typical August afternoon in the Wisconsin countryside, are pretty average. We experience almost the whole of our lives as common days made up of small things and ordinary, oft-repeated transactions. The repetition of these events constitutes nearly our whole experience with one another and our daily reality. I've come to believe that this kind of averageness points, not to mediocrity but to a healing energy, a greater reality that flows through the veins of our simple daily encounters. This kind of averageness can honestly inform our goals and values as we make important life choices.

Excitement, ambition, and a thousand questionable causes may elevate us occasionally, but they will never replace the connectedness of sharing a meal with a friend or holding the hand of someone who has received a breast cancer diagnosis. In the end, the real healing we experience comes not from what we acquire or achieve but from our willingness to be transformed—transformed as in the process of discovering the truth about ourselves and about where we stand in relation to the world. By this process, we take off the covers and reveal the light and success that are already living within us.

We ultimately are invited not just to attain; we're invited to set off on foot toward the August season of our fruition. We are invited to walk on the holy ground of our human experience, the unspectacular and sometimes painful experience of becoming available to life and to one another. The true meaning of life, after all, lies hidden behind the ordinary. It speaks in quiet tones, not in high drama but in the average. And sometimes we find our way to a more rewarding plan when we adjust our course before looking outside for someone to fix it.

Consider This: Autoimmunity and Women

Autoimmune diseases affect approximately 8 percent of the population, 75 percent of whom are women. Named a major women's health issue by the Office of Research on Women's Health at the National Institutes of Health, autoimmunity serves as the underlying cause of more than one hundred serious chronic illnesses. These diseases occur when the body's immune system becomes misdirected and attacks the very organ it was designed to protect. When this occurs, the body manufactures immune cells, called T-cells, and autoantibodies, which attack the body's own cells and organs. These misguided T-cells and autoantibodies contribute to many autoimmune diseases that implicate many medical specialties, including rheumatology, endocrinology, hematology, neurology, cardiology, gastroenterology, and dermatology.

Estimates suggest that autoimmune diseases are responsible for more than one hundred billion dollars in direct health care costs annually. While there has been little coordinated scientific attention to the underlying causes of these diseases and why they are more prevalent in women, research is looking at both the biological and psychosocial factors that might contribute to these debilitating diseases. Jill's ulcerative colitis, like its sister condition, Crohn's disease, is treated as an autoimmune disease.[5]

While change often begins with pain, pain is not necessarily where it ends. It is also true that today's prevailing media messages tell us to avoid pain at all costs. We learn to deny, medicate, avoid, ignore, and otherwise hide from pain. Additionally, we load our days with things that create disharmony.

- Describe a time when a painful event or situation caused you to make a change for the better.
- Explain the outcome of that change and its effect on the quality of your life.

Which of the following interferes most with your sense of harmony and well-being? Do you
- worry chronically?

---

[5] See American Autoimmune Related Diseases Association at aarda.org.

- neglect fun?
- refuse to waste time well?
- take yourself too seriously?
- blame and complain?
- overlook the power of gratitude?
- work excessively?
- shortchange friendships due to your busyness?

20

Why Spirituality Matters

We are not human beings having a spiritual experience. We are spiritual beings having a human experience.
—Pierre Teilhard de Chardin

When a friend or colleague in the midst of a crisis starts asking me questions such as "Why? How did this happen?" or "What does this mean?" I know that we are about to have a conversation about God. Whether that God resides within a traditional religious institution, an Alcoholics Anonymous meeting, or a meditative search for happiness, spiritual engagement matters. A rich spiritual life feeds our capacity to weather change and find satisfaction in the ordinary, everyday experiences of our lives. I experienced a moving example of this spiritual energy at work while visiting an AA meeting in a local homeless shelter. A drug counselor had invited me to join the group for dinner and the meeting that followed.

The first meeting began with a small circle of homeless men listening attentively as the counselor announced the assignment for the coming week. The faces might have belonged to anyone anywhere. From professionals with postgraduate degrees to the old and sickly, they came to the gospel mission from offices, street corners, and jails. They called themselves late-stage chronic alcoholics, and they were the men who huddled beneath city bridges in the December cold, sipping kerosene. Many had gone again and again through local detox centers and shelters. All were searching for a reason to hope.

The counselor had asked them each to write a prayer. Everyone managed to cobble together some words for the next meeting—everyone except one older man. Each time the counselor asked how things were coming along with the assignment, he slowly shook his head and stared at the floor. Years on the streets, immersed in alcohol and gloom, had left him an empty vessel.

Week after week, the group met; the members of this tiny recovering community shared personal anecdotes and harrowing experiences. One evening when the ragged group assembled once more. The counselor again asked the man if he'd brought his prayer.

"Yes" was the reply, much to everyone's surprise. He then pulled a crumpled bit of paper from his pocket and offered up a six-word entreaty: "Whoever made me, keep me safe."

The core of this petition disclosed much about the man who prayed it. It also discloses much about any of us who have faced a life-altering crisis and are searching for healing and connection with a source of strength beyond self. Some would call this a spiritual search. Others might say it was an epiphany. Whatever one chooses to call this moment, it encompassed a light that began to reveal this man's path toward recovery.

Spirituality is a popular concept, mentioned over and over in self-help literature, complementary medicine, and popular cultural. Yet spiritual language has often been confined to the recovery and religious communities, and this diminishes the strength and fullness of its meaning. We often read about all the things a person can do to improve his or her spiritual health, but rarely do we hear about what it means to be a spiritually whole person; in fact, even though spirituality lies at the heart of AA's Twelve Steps and most world religions, misunderstanding of the term abounds. For example, it's not often pointed out that the Twelve Steps of AA simply provide a means of nurturing spiritual constructs such as simplicity, honesty, trust, and humility—all basic, necessary ingredients of our human relationships and our feelings of well-being.

Each of us, as a distinct and separate person, possesses a sense of isolation, of living within the boundaries of the self. Yet we also have a basic need to believe that we belong in the world in some meaningful way. We inherently understand that we can transcend our separate selves. In part, the term "spirituality" is used to address this universal human longing for intimacy, community, and order. To be spiritually complete implies that we understand our purpose in the world. To be spiritually whole means we have examined central issues of life, such as our understanding of self and how we relate to others and the world in which we live.

The spiritual dimension is difficult to define, let alone measure. It does not meet the objective criteria needed for scientific analysis. To some, its subjective manifestations might appear to involve wishful thinking, pathological projection, or the abandonment of rational analysis. In fact, it's is the spiritual dimension that ultimately guides us in our search for purpose.

Consider This: A Mini-Guide to the Term "Spirituality"

The term "spirituality" is applied mainly to subjective phenomena. A number of concepts, however, help to capture some elements of spirituality. The following encompass some (not all) of these elements, which can influence one's health, happiness, and capacity to cope with change:

- *A belief in some intrinsic meaning or order in the universe*
- *A faith that humanity and creation are inherently good*
- *An understanding that the force hidden in creation is a loving, present, and active energy*
- *A trust that this active energy behind creation could be called God or a Higher Power*
- *A willingness to accept what is (this is not to be confused with grudging resignation or with approval of evil)*
- *A fundamental expectation of future good*
- *An ability to find peace of mind in an imperfect, ambiguous world*

- *A capacity to make peace with the knowledge that one's own personality is imperfect, although acceptable*

Finally, growth or integration of one's inner or spiritual self produces a peaceful internal environment that nourishes flexibility, creativity, acceptance, trust, forgiveness, love, compassion, and hope—all those assets that help us transition to more healthful directions and experiences.

"Spirit," derived from Latin, signifies breath or wind. It's basic to humankind, a vital element of our individual and collective humanity. Treatment professionals have long known that addiction affects every part of a person, including that person's spirit. Thus, when someone begins to seek the fullness of living at a spiritual level, he or she also begins to recover from addiction.

A "spiritual awakening" tends to help a person see and feel things she could not see or feel before. A spiritual awakening opens the door to knowledge previously hidden. This is how the Twelve Steps of Alcoholics Anonymous help people let go of their addictive selves and recognize their spiritual task of cultivating friendships and intimacy through simplicity, honesty, trust, and humility. It is at the level of spirit that one finds strength and identity through fellowship with others. This is the place where power comes from something larger than self, a source of wisdom that can guide us as we grow and change.

A spirituality defined in these terms encompasses a spirituality of movement toward completion or wholeness. It accentuates companionship—friend with friend, helping, sharing, celebrating, and even despairing. The spiritual essence moves us toward a relationship with the universe, with others, and with ourselves. It asks, "Who am I? Where do I find meaning and purpose in life? How do I bond with others?"

A spirituality of wholeness invites the deepest forms of human healing. This healing lives in our present and daily experience of one another. It says,

"I will help someone for no other reason than that she needs help. I will live out a life of compassion as a vital act of creation. I will make justice by acting mercifully."

This spirituality offers free and cordial emptiness for others to enter, a space where souls can get acquainted. It shatters our illusions of having it all together, of having control, or of attaining personal perfection. Finally, it challenges us to walk with hope on an uncharted footpath called life.

A spirituality of wholeness speaks of simplicity. To be human means to be in touch with the earth and all who inhabit it, to be reconciled and made whole. The humble host knows that each guest carries precious gifts. This spirituality says that upon discovering our unique nature, we also find that we are one with the homeless man. His prayer could be our prayer.

"Whoever made me, keep me safe."

In fact, this is a prayer of belief that we are indeed part of a sweeping plan that includes much more than our own dilemmas and our own space. This kind of trust says that we can search our hearts, make amends, be reconciled, and embrace a change in our journeys whenever we choose.

- What is your image of God or Higher Power?
- How has your perception of life changed as a result of change?
- Do you feel you have an adequate support system?
- Do you have a space in which you can be vulnerable and free of judgment?
- Do you feel you have adequate spiritual support?
- What is the most important thing you have learned in life?
- Do you look forward to the future with enthusiasm?

21

Noah's Notes—Laugh and Let Go

Madam reported to me that her First Born purchased a home—not one of those gargantuan manors that sprang up from the middle of a once charming pasture but a 1951 bungalow. This is good, since the First Born knows less than a crumb about home maintenance. It's also good, because it marks the beginning of a new era for Madam—that of an empty-nester, at least technically.

Night one: the first phone call came at midnight.

"How much is it going to rain?" demanded the First Born, who never guessed that weather reports were a big deal up here on the Minnesota tundra.

"I couldn't tell you," Madam mumbled from under the Hairball Pets that share her pillow. "Why do you ask? More to the point, why do you ask at midnight?"

"It's just wrong," moaned the First Born.

"Yes, It does seem a bit off to ring at midnight, requesting a meteorology report," offered Madam with a yawn. "Have you tried turning on your TV or phoning the state climatology department?"

The call ended with Madam's assurances that a little rain would not extinguish the 1951 bungalow. It did, however, deposit a smidge of water on the basement floor. This prompted a second call.

"How do I get rid of water in the basement?" wailed the First Born. "Should I call the home inspector? How about the seller? She never told me this would happen. Do I need a plumber? Do you have a wet vac? Should I contact the DNR?"

"Just wipe it up with a towel," sighed Madam. "To my knowledge, the DNR does not manage wet basements unless you're harboring wildlife or growing pot down there."

Day two, call number three: "Do you have a hammer? How about a Phillips screwdriver? By the way, what is a Phillips screwdriver?" queried the First Born. "I bought a vacuum and it requires some minor assembly."

Oh dear. "Have you read the instructions?" Madam asked the daughter who could barely turn the lights out without a tutorial.

"Also, the fridge is making grinding sounds that frighten the cats," declared the First Born. "Do you have a cooler to store my frozen food? That's it; I'm calling the realtor."

"I'm sure she will appreciate hearing how well you're getting along in your new home," replied Madam.

Day three, call four: "I'm locked out."

"How is it that you're locked out at 5:00 a.m.?" Madam asked evenly.

"It was the cats that kept me awake. They aren't adjusting well. I need to call a pet behaviorist," sobbed the First Born. "It's dark out."

"I see that," soothed Madam. "I'll come get you."

"And please bring coffee," begged the First Born.

Dressed in her pajamas and a pair of rubber Wellies, Madam pulled up to the curb and observed her First Born wrenching an oversized cat kennel out the porch door and stumbling down the front steps.

"How did you happen to bring the cat along?" Madam quizzed.

"He might have to go number two, and I figured you have cat litter at your house," explained the First Born. "I'm out of litter."

I'm not surprised. "Do you think you should put the house back on the market and move home?" queried Madam tentatively.

"Maybe," said the First Born.
"Or maybe not," added Madam.

22

Robin Savage Aspires to Accept What Is

Acceptance doesn't mean resignation; it means understanding that something is what it is and that there's got to be a way through it.

—Michael J. Fox

The RAND Corporation estimates that by the year 2020, 48.3 percent of the US population will be living with a chronic health or condition.[6]

These ongoing, generally incurable illnesses and conditions include heart disease, asthma, cancer, diabetes, and, in the case of stand-up comedian Robin Savage, a nervous system disorder that causes rhythmic shaking, called *essential tremor*. Essential tremor can affect almost any part of the body, but the trembling occurs most often in the hands. Robin used to look at her condition as an embarrassment problem, not a health problem. Today, she describes her relationship with essential tremor as a journey that has led her from hiding it to trying to fix it and, finally, to accepting it.

"I used to think I was the only person who had this problem," said Robin. "When I was a kid, I didn't have a lot going for me. I was a tomboy with unruly hair and no interest in being a girly-girl." Essential tremor added one more

---

[6] rand.org/topics/chronic-diseases-and-conditions.html

challenge for her, a challenge she has faced for as long as she can remember.

But she was always funny.

Whether acting out an impression of Dan Aykroyd's Jimmy Carter or imitating Mork from the *Mork and Mindy* TV show, Robin's quirky personality set her apart from her peers. And her uncontrollable trembling did not elicit many invitations to play games like egg toss or Jenga.

Diagnosed at an early age, Robin remembers the doctors telling her parents she had hypoglycemia, though eliminating sugar from her diet brought no improvement. She kept hoping she would outgrow the tremors, though that never happened. Instead, she found herself despising the forces within her body that tried to dictate what she could do or not do. No surprise that classmates teased her unmercifully. Adults and children alike constantly commented on her quivering hands. By the time she got to high school, she was convinced that all this trembling must mean she was an alcoholic.

She joined the Forensic and Debate Society in high school, hoping it would provide the avenue that validated her gift of humor. Instead, it only earned her the "I Tried" award for five years in a row. Even her clever creations in the fables and storytelling division netted last place. The judges interpreted her shaking as anxiety. When the Drama Club decided to present "An Evening of One Acts," however, Robin tried out for a lead role. She gave it her best effort, got the part, and loved performing in the two-weekends run.

"It's been thirty years, and I still remember the huge laughs at that audition," she said. "I even asked the drama teacher about my shaking, and she said as long as I had my lines memorized and my blocking correct, no one could really notice it from the stage." While that might not have been the most helpful answer, it was an encouraging one for a young woman eager to perform.

Following her performance, one of the teachers said that watching Robin was like watching a young Carol Burnett, which was enough to encourage Robin to do more. Over time, she found herself performing in front of all types of audiences, making people laugh, even if it wasn't always theater or stand-up comedy. For example, she spent five years shaping a dull, call-center–training job into an amusing exercise for her newly hired trainees.

Life marched on. Eventually, Robin married, settled in Tampa, had two children, and enjoyed her life as a stay-at-home mom. But comedy still beckoned. Then one day, while researching a toddler music or dance class for her two-year-old son, she came across an adult stand-up comedy class offered by Tampa's Straz Performing Arts Center. Realizing that this was a now-or-never proposition, she signed up.

At first, she didn't tell anyone, including her husband, that it was a comedy class. According to Robin, she wanted to keep an "escape route" handy, like the "coward" exits available in a roller-coaster waiting line. Once she began performing in class, she moved on to an open microphone appearance, and then to another. Stand-up comedy for her soon shifted from a hobby to a calling. She began emceeing and occasionally headlining on a variety of stages. All this confirmed what she had known for years: engaging people in laughter was very addicting.

Meanwhile, her tremors continued. She tried holding the microphone with one hand, then two hands, and even took it out of her hands and placed it in a stationary position. She wrote and performed material about shaking. She also tried going on stage without uttering a word about it.

"When I first went on stage, my whole body was shaking, and I think I scared people," said Robin. "I still deal with the tremors in my daily life, but when I have a microphone in my hand and hear the laughter, nothing else seems to matter. It's like the happiness of soul trumps the limitations of my body."

Today, Robin finds herself transitioning from an active life in stand-up comedy to an equally active life focused more on family and home. She's ready to take a break from late-night acts and accommodate her busy children.

"I feel a little conflict," she admitted. "On one hand, I want to be accessible as a mom. On the hand, I want my kids to see that I'm setting an example for them by working hard to pursue my dreams."

This does not mean she's retired, just reaching a comfortable level of acceptance of both her physical and professional situation. She has redirected her activities to blogging, video production, acting, publishing a book titled *Stand Up and Be a Lady*, and other creative projects that keep her closer to home. Another item on her to-do list: rethinking the kind of comedy she would like to pursue next.

According to Robin, in comedy, one typically faces competition that performs some pretty bawdy acts. "I think I'd like to do something nicer," she offered. Eight years of following raunchy acts have encouraged her to consider a refreshed approach to humor, as well as the venues and audiences she aims to entertain. She recently attended a luncheon featuring journalist, motivational speaker, and long-distance swimmer Diana Nyad that confirmed her feelings about making a change. The event left Robin questioning if it wasn't time for her to set new goals, including performing in attractive settings in front of courteous, well-intentioned audiences.

"I've been wondering, why not come up with funny yet more tasteful material and a nice clean place to perform it?" she explained.

In fact, Robin's work has reached well beyond comedy clubs to the Tampa Crisis Center, where she has delivered her stand-up humor to an audience coping with the devastating trauma of sexual assault or abuse, domestic violence, financial distress, substance abuse, and much more. She also has won a Best Actress award for a comedy short that she cowrote in the 2014 Saint Pete Comedy Film Festival. In addition, Robin remains an active participant in the International Tremor Foundation.

"The big picture of my life is pretty amazing," she acknowledged. "I have a great family, a few people I can call true friends, and a gift for making others laugh."

She also exemplifies a level of acceptance that helps transform her journey from one set of goals and expectations to the next.

Consider This: Acceptance, the Sister of Hope

Acceptance sometimes gets confused with grudging resignation. Though that might accompany one's initial feelings about a loss, injustice, or a medical problem, it seems that a more genuine acceptance is a different matter. Acceptance, as a point of wholeness, means accepting conditions as they are, with all the injustices and hard-to-swallow suffering that comes with them. Acceptance also implies

- an assured sense that one can transcend the present situation.
- an attitude toward life, not just an occasional feeling to turn to when we need it.
- a disposition that says the future is an open one and holds possibility.
- a sense of and belief in future good, that future good can occur even in the face of a current condition or deprivation.
- the capacity to see oneself in a larger landscape.

23

Find Meaning in the Dark

Deep into that darkness peering, long I stood there, wondering, fearing, doubting, dreaming dreams no mortal ever dared to dream before.

—Edgar Allan Poe

The terms "cure" and "healing" signify two distinct avenues to the same end: becoming whole. Used in this context, "cure" pertains to specific acts of scientific intervention. "Healing," on the other hand, points to a set of possibilities that all of us can bring to a seemingly untenable situation. While a healing approach might not always change an outcome or prevent a loss, it can improve our own or another's sense of resolve. A healing attitude encompasses assets such as patience and our capacity to listen to the voice within our hearts. Each has the power to light up the path ahead or even the root cellar below.

Once, while listening to a psychologist speak with a group of adults living with depression and anxiety, I was surprised when he read them a story that sounded like a children's story, though it produced a resounding response from his listeners. The subject was a narcissus bulb, and the story went like this:

A child once visited a garden with her grandmother. The two of them wandered hand in hand among the ancient beech trees and on narrow paths banked with foxglove, roses, and delicate Turk's cap lilies. The old woman told her granddaughter of many mysterious and healing properties of flowers. She spoke of roots and petals crushed into secret potions, exotic balms, magic elixirs, and bewitching perfumes.

Eventually, they came upon a willow basket filled with flower bulbs. The grandmother invited the girl to select one of the bulbs so that she might take it home and plant it in her own garden. After inspecting the snarled clump of roots, the girl made her choice, and slipped it into the pocket of her dress.

"That is a very special bulb you've chosen," said her grandmother. "It's called a narcissus, and you must cultivate it with great care in order to extract all of its beauty and healing power. The first thing you must do when you get home is hide it in a dark place and leave it there undisturbed until it begins to sprout. Only when the bulb has sent out roots can you plant it among the rest of the flowers." The child thought this rather odd but promised her grandmother she would do as she instructed.

After placing the bulb in a mixture of moss and damp clay, they set it out of sight on a cellar shelf. But the child could not resist occasionally opening the door to see if the narcissus had started to grow. "Occasionally" soon became every hour and sometimes even more. Each morning she sprang from her bed, raced down the steps to the dark root cellar, and peered through the shadows, hoping to see some sign of life. Each day brought greater disappointment than the last.

She sulked. She cried. She wailed to her grandmother, convinced that she had brought home a dead bulb. The old woman listened quietly but only counseled patience. One morning, while the household still slept, the child crept down to the cellar and removed the bulb from its hiding place. She washed the clay from its smooth onionlike skin and examined the surface with a reading glass. Nothing.

Finally, after weeks of watching and wishing, the child gave up hope. Surely she would never see her narcissus bloom. Bored with waiting and certain that the bulb would never grow, she stopped checking on it. *How silly*, she thought, *to think that such an ugly little thing could ever turn into something beautiful, especially in the dark.*

Then one day, her grandmother called to her from the bottom of the cellar steps. "Look here," said the old woman brightly. "Something seems to have happened to your bulb."

Her granddaughter gasped in disbelief when she saw the little pot of soil. Something indeed had happened. The bulb had sprouted. From its top protruded a soft green nub and underneath, a thick clump of roots. Sure enough the narcissus was alive.

It grew quickly then, flourishing in the dark, just as her grandmother had promised. Soon the child moved it from the cellar to a spot in the garden bed reserved for the first flowers of spring.

To this day the little bulb continues to thrive, though each winter it retires to a dark and mysterious place from which it draws energy, so that it might grow and bloom the following spring.

The animated group discussion that followed this story surprised me. It was abundantly clear that everyone identified with more than just the darkness. They also felt the energy of possibilities that frequently visited them in the dark.

For these individuals, as for all of us, growth often takes place in darkness. Darkness is where simple wishes are transformed into enduring dreams. Peace and healing meet in the unlit corners of the human heart. It is the winter days and long nights of our lives that invite us to send down roots, to grow in courage and hope. When we accept this invitation to wait patiently in our darkness, we accept the prospect of a new quest toward a season of hope.

Consider This: Waiting for Hope

The idea of hope and growth taking place in darkness seems counterintuitive. Nonetheless, many people who have faced the loss of a dream have discovered that dark places can also nurture a new vision. The human heart keeps many hidden treasures that can be missed in the daylight hustle toward success and happiness. Perhaps the most important thing to remember during these pivotal points is to keep on questioning.

Think of a time when you experienced an unexpected turn of events—exciting or disturbing—that plummeted you into a dark place.

How did this make you feel? Helpless? Anxious? Hopeless? Guilty?

Upon reflection, what personal assets eventually helped bring you back to a brighter spot?

- Patience?
- Adaptability?
- Resourcefulness?
- Faith?
- Other?

24

Celebrate, Large and Small

The more you praise and celebrate your life, the more there is in life to celebrate.

—Oprah Winfrey

A couple of years ago, I visited an old family friend, Joan Pearson, who was piloting her elder years on a small sheep farm near Milwaukee. Upon my arrival, she marched me outside for an agricultural tour. We began with a brief hike to the edge of a pond, where a flock of Canada geese eyed me up as if I were on a Homeland Security watch list. Joan shooed them off with a broom and assured me I would be safe from any untoward goose assaults if I stayed close to her. I did just that. She then introduced me to her three-year-old granddaughter, Christine, who proceeded to lead the way on our tour.

When we reached our destination, Christine climbed to the top of a rock pile and began sorting her collection of quartz and agates. Occasionally, she tossed a small stone into the pond below, prompting harsh words from the geese. Four Bernese mountain dogs loped about on the mountain of stones left over from last spring's pond dredging. A chorus of barks rained down on Christine as she placidly sorted her treasures. The dogs careened in and out of the water, retrieving rocks as Joan urged her granddaughter to come down and join us for a hike along the river. With that, Christine turned a somersault in the mud, warbled a verse of "Oh! Susanna," and skipped ahead of us with the dogs close behind. Joan obviously encouraged this kind of merrymaking from grandchildren. She knew how to celebrate, large and small.

The driveway to her home offered the first clues to Joan's sense of fun. A sign next to the mailbox identified the farm as the Shepherd's Patch, an allusion to her late husband, an Episcopalian bishop. A tilting flagpole served as the centerpiece for an array of toys, garden hoses, and unidentifiable items of clothing. The front porch, strewn with dog dishes and croquet mallets, also provided a stage for children's dramatic productions. Clay pots filled with twigs lay among old baking utensils and a snow shovel. Two church pews and a wheelbarrow leaned against the garage. The garage looked pretty empty, as everything of any substance resided on the front porch. A sprinkling of garden trowels and a pitchfork hinted at Joan's obsession with gardening and Cotswold sheep.

Our next stop was the barn. It really did house two Cotswold rams named Willie Billy and Billy Willie, more reminders of the dear departed, "Very Reverend William." A couple of dozen startled ewes swung their heads up as the dogs ran through their pasture, dragging some part of a deer carcass. Joan's toolshed, crammed with wire and stakes, offered a backdrop for a dead pickup truck that listed gently over its front tires. A faded sign nailed to the cow shed marked the property as a licensed game farm, where Joan hatched pheasant in cooperation with the Wisconsin Department of Natural Resources. It was her relationship with the DNR that produced the pond-dredging project. This eventually became home to hundreds of small trout and a spa for the dogs. No wonder the grandchildren sobbed when their parents retrieved them from such a hotbed of entertainment.

Joan's "costumes" varied throughout the day, from barn to garden to marketing apparel. That morning she wore a lemon-yellow T-shirt and blue knit pants. She also donned a baseball cap with an orange bird's-beak visor. Black patent-leather flats trimmed in colored buttons and floral print anklets completed her ensemble. Some might have called her eccentric, though the kids surely saw her as an elderly Peter Pan. She carried a grocery bag filled with asparagus that she and Christine had collected earlier. The combination of colors and sounds at the Shepherd's Patch reflected Joan's unfettered tribute to life's simplest pleasures. Yet behind all this fun stood a woman who possessed character strengths and virtues that served a greater purpose than her own personal goals. Persistence, faith, and curiosity defined her life of many colors.

She was a terrible driver, famous for ferrying lambs to the veterinarian in her old Volkswagen bus. A woman with more than a few opinions, her deafening bellow could send a brave soul scampering for cover. She once hosted a New Year's Eve party during which the family cockatiel made a three-point landing in the punch bowl. Joan simply swept up the bowl, plus bathing bird, and scurried to the kitchen. Barely missing a beat, she rinsed and dried the cockatiel, plucked a few feathers out of the punch and returned it to the serving table. Why bother guests with cumbersome explanations? Visiting Joan was brilliant, mostly because she extracted joy out of the most common things—not that a punch-swilling cockatiel was so common.

The word "celebration" usually implies music, dancing, and laughter—holidays and entertainment that help us temporarily forget the difficulties of life. We think of immersing ourselves in an atmosphere of excitement and pleasant unreality. Clearly, Joan loved a good party, but from her vantage point, celebration also meant an acceptance of life and the awareness of its preciousness. Celebration, for her, happened where fear and love, joy and sorrow, tears and smiles, and young and old could coexist with some measure of harmony. She viewed life as treasured, not only because it could be seen, touched, and tasted but because it would be gone one day.

Watching Joan with Christine that morning, I saw a woman who had experienced her own sorrows. Her husband had died a decade earlier. At age eighty-four, she was entering her fifth year of trials and treatments for lymphoma. Lost bone density and the crippling effects of a deteriorated spine caused her pain. Yet she continued choosing to live in the present and to go with whatever life handed her on that day. Christine and her other grandchildren invited her to be with them here and now. Their uninhibited expressions of affection and willingness to receive it pulled her directly into the moment and invited her to celebrate life where it could be found. Neither old age nor physical challenges would have caused her to tell her doctor that she was in "bad" health. She had a strong community of family and friends and a focal point somewhere outside of herself. And—perhaps most vital—she lived her life from a center of love.

Today, five years later, Joan continues to perk along. She still drives, much to her family's dismay—not because she can no longer rise to the challenges of driving, but because she has been denting cars and backing through garage doors for some fifty years. Besides, her head barely reaches the top of the steering wheel, and we can only guess what she sees or doesn't see on the road. Once or twice a year, she leaves the car behind and visits her older sister, Ruth, in California, marching through airports on her own, enjoying a little change of venue.

Speaking of travel, Joan's daughters and I once carried her like the Queen of Hearts in her bathing suit and plunked her in a Colorado hot spring. That same trip, we gave her a first-time tour of the Brass Ass Casino in Cripple Creek, where she tested the slots and won seven hundred dollars. After being served a *winning* drink called "Naked on the Beach," she gave the money to her daughter to start an inner-city youth computer program in a Boston library. More recently, we helped Joan into a kayak and paddled around Sanibel Island's Ding Darling Bird Sanctuary. While I fussed about encountering an alligator, she paddled on, undaunted by every manner of creature that slithered past us.

She's an avid reader. Her nightstand sags under the weight of publications, from the history of Ireland to Wensleydale cheese. Each day finds her with a full schedule and an occasional nap among friends or wherever it's convenient. Her spirit of discovery feeds her sense of whimsy. She's confident that "the fun is in the doing."

Knowing Joan and many other elders who live with debilitating health conditions, I have concluded that health is sometimes a matter of value judgment—a judgment first made by a patient but on which both health care professional and patient must agree. For example, an elderly woman or man might go to a doctor's office with a list of health problems, from diabetes to arthritis. If that person were Joan, she probably would tell her doctor that she was getting out and around, could do the things she enjoyed, and felt quite healthy, thank you very much.

Definitions of health abound, though most would agree on certain basic elements. For example, good health includes an absence of significant disease and of excessive conflict, pain, or anxiety. Health also includes a sense of well-being—the ability to function effectively and in a reasonably good mood. A definition of health also suggests a degree of self-discipline and balance, and it includes a capacity to love others and feel connected to them.

Illness, on the other hand, begins with the absence—partial or complete—of this valuable asset called health. The brokenness of illness involves threats to one's feelings of connection and meaning. Illness can interfere with one's security, challenge one's sense of control over one's destiny, and produce feelings of alienation from family and community. Pain and loss of function can disrupt one's ordinary means of making contact, thus intensifying detachment from everyday routines.

Like health, illness holds different meanings for different people. I've met patients and families who have treated their illnesses as an enemy, to be fought with every weapon in the medical arsenal. For some, it became a strategy through which they manipulated others. And others saw illness as an irreparable loss or damage. In almost every case, the meaning of wellness or illness related directly to a person's perception of her or his life.

Women like Joan seem to transcend infirmities with an innate self-healing capacity that lies somewhere outside of science and technology—somewhere within her being. As she steers through what likely is her final life plan, she has reached a level of reconciliation. This reconciliation engenders wholeness for her and joy for each of us who have known her.

Consider This: Life Is a Narrative Worth Sharing

At some point along the way, I began to realize that life is not just a journey but a narrative—a winding trail of words and symbols from childhood to maturity and from youth to age; from innocence to awareness and from ignorance to knowing; from foolishness to discretion and then, perhaps, to wisdom; from weakness to strength or from strength to weakness; from health to sickness and back (we pray) to health; from offense to forgiveness; from loneliness to love; from joy to gratitude; from pain to compassion and from grief to understanding; from fear to faith; from defeat to reconciliation ... until, looking backward or ahead, we finally see that victory lies not at some high place along the way but in having made the journey, stage by stage.

25

Noah's Notes—Friendship, the Real Meaning behind Deer Hunting

Laughter is not at all a bad beginning for a friendship,
and it is far the best ending for one.
—Oscar Wilde

One thing I've learned since moving from Oklahoma to flyover country up North: never under estimate the lure of deer hunting season. I'm referring to that time of year when every buck-stalker in possession of a Cabela's credit card slips into blaze orange and dons a camo headlamp for a few days. It's a taxidermist's dream and high season at the Buck Knuckle Saloon.

"So what's the meaning of this gun-toting quest for a multipointed hat rack?" I asked Madam. As a guy who thought *conceal and carry* was what you did when you nicked the last slice of carrot cake, I was confused. She rolled her eyes, as she often does when I ask culturally insensitive questions.

"Noah, you've missed the point. This isn't about deer or hunting. It's about old friends getting together to raise a toast to old friends."

A fine idea, but it struck me that old friends could accomplish the same thing over a cup of coffee and a slice of banana cream pie at the Norske Nook. I thought it best not to mention this thought.

Madam presented me with a deer hunting tutorial. It all started when her father, a retired judge, and three of his Depression era cronies hatched a plan to make one last trip to deer camp—for old time's sake. Apparently, these guys had been making a North Woods pilgrimage together since 1945. Incidentally, Madam couldn't recall the Judge or any of the others coming home with a departed deer strapped to the roof of his car.

Anyhoo, on opening day, the senior hunters loaded Alden Jacobson's Dodge Minivan with the required Cuban cigars, toilet paper, Bicycle playing cards, cribbage board, and a large rolling cooler full of groceries. Alden traditionally planned the menu, and the Judge traditionally complained that it included too much of his wife, Myrtle's, krumkake and not enough steak. Meanwhile, the Judge, who had spent decades dispatching orders from his bench, appointed retired police detective Walt Shwank to help Alden cook. He then assigned old Ed Witzig to tend the fire and the mousetraps. Ed also brought a handful of bungee cords to keep nighttime prowlers out of the garbage cans. As for the Judge, he volunteered to manage artillery.

It took most of the morning, but the guys finally managed to stuff all their supplies and sleeping bags into Alden's minivan. With everyone on board, Alden pointed north to the favorite hideout, Camp Rum Dumb.

After stopping once for coffee in Hayward and a second time to pick up a bottle of bourbon at the Dew Drop Inn, they pulled into camp. Everyone agreed that they should unload the perishables and check the propane tank before setting out to trail trophy bucks. According to Madam, only the Judge and Alden carried guns, which seemed like a blessing. Armed with binoculars, Ed and Walt tottered down the fire lane behind the other two. Walt brought a couple of egg salad sandwiches to share, and he and Ed ate their lunch while regaling one another with Camp Rum Dumb tales from years past.

There was the time Ed fell out of his deer stand and landed on a sleeping bull snake. Then, in 1965, a skunk family took up residence under the kitchen sink, forcing Alden to move his food prep outside to the grill. These mishaps, as well as a couple of stovetop fires, shed light on why nobody ever got around to locating deer. It was beginning to sound like a chickadee group.

So once more they hit the trail hoping to finally change their luck. When an hour passed with no deer sightings, the fearsome foursome decided to go back to camp and set up housekeeping. Ed secured the garbage can lids from wayward raccoons, while Alden and Walt cooked up a meatloaf and mashed potatoes. Ed and the Judge played a couple of hands of gin rummy. It was a perfect day, the Judge later reported to Madam. After dinner, a crackling fire in the fireplace and a drop of bourbon topped off their stroll down memory lane. At midnight they all retired to their sleeping bags.

About an hour later, a clatter arose from the kitchen.

"What is it?" whispered Walt, groping for his glasses. "Who's in here? Come out here with your hands above your head!" No response.

The Judge clicked on his flashlight to have a look. Nobody felt compelled to try to capture the intruder. "What's going on out there?" he bellowed. Just then, the flashlight beam landed upon a startled weasel with a salad fork in its mouth. It glared into the light from atop the kitchen table.

"Well, I'll be," croaked Ed. "He must have liked the meatloaf."

Nobody moved a whisker, including the weasel. Finally, the deafening silence was broken with an equally deafening explosion. Walt had packed his old service revolver and chose that moment to shoot a hole in the ceiling. Not much clear thinking behind this approach, unless he thought the weasel would see the new skylight and find its way out.

No such luck. The weasel darted off the table but not out the hole. By this time, the Judge's flashlight had tumbled to the floor with a loud clank and rolled under a bed. This was followed with a chorus of "Shoo, shoo! Get out!" as the weasel rounded the cabin and rocketed into Alden's duffel bag. Given the rumpus on the other side of the room, they could tell that the weasel had made a dive into Ed's sleeping bag—right alongside Ed. What followed was proof that an eighty-year-old man can run as fast as Jesse Owens when joined in bed by a fork-wielding weasel.

I was almost afraid to ask Madam what happened next.

"Well, Noah you'll be glad to know that the weasel made it out of Camp Rum Dum alive," she reported. "And believe it or not, old Ed suffered nothing more than a twisted ankle from sprinting out the door in his skivvies."

Everyone was relieved that Walt's gun made it back to the holster with no more action. The Judge promptly locked the sidearm in the trunk of Alden's minivan to avoid any repeat performances. And so the four old friends had a fine time deer hunting without firing a shot—more or less. The weasel lived. Camp Rum Dumb suffered a little cosmetic damage, though small wildlife probably appreciated the new cabin entrance.

Oddly, this little caper was starting to make perfect sense to me. The oldsters might not have bagged a buck, and they no doubt faced plenty of worries and limitations that came with their aging, but they sure knew how to have fun with their friends.

Consider This: Reenergize Relationships

How easy it is to expect our important relationships to perk along without much change or attention to detail on our part. Good friends stay good friends forever. Work colleagues promise to keep connected, even when they take another job, move to another city, or retire. Spouses remain sane and steady through the years. Much of the time, these trusted friend and partner relationships flow along smoothly without the need for excessive care. On the other hand, I have found that all relationships that matter require consideration and care, no matter how robust they might appear on the surface.

Strong relationships with supportive friends, helpmates, and colleagues provide a foundation on which we thrive at every age. High-school chums, college classmates, intimate partners, new mothers, or retired deer hunters—no matter who we are or in what stage of the journey we happen to be traveling, relationships we care about need care and attention.

Relationships affect everything from our understanding of truth to our level of self-esteem. They influence our motivation to engage in life and our desire to pursue our dreams. While it is easy to take close relationships for granted, it is vital to feed those relationships to keep them strong and well. Consider the following ideas for adding new life to important relationships:

- Express sincere appreciation of another. Remind that person of how much she or he means to you. Send a note. Focus on individual strengths and achievements, and offer genuine compliments. Acknowledge this person's positive contributions to your day.

- Set dates to spend time in the company of people whose relationships you value. If they have moved, offer to come for a visit or meet them halfway. Choose something new to do together. Pack a lunch to share and head for the zoo or museum of natural history. Review your calendar regularly, making certain you keep appointments with those who hold a place of prominence in your life.

- Communicate often with those close to you. Find times to connect, and set those times aside from daily routines. Stop talking about how busy you are. E-mail someone. Send him or her a photo of your new cat. Take a coffee break together, and use your time to listen and speak of things that matter to both of you. No whining.

- Consider ways of strengthening your spiritual and cultural activities, individually and together. Attend a presentation within and beyond your faith traditions or political preferences. Visit a public garden. Hike with a naturalist.

Set aside a day for a bird-watching expedition. Rent a canoe or kayak for an afternoon.

- Make your relationships a high priority. Despite busy schedules, investing time and energy in relationships is so fulfilling and makes a real difference in the quality of our lives. Listen to another's needs. Assure someone that you care for her or his well-being and plan to be there during times of difficulty as well as times of fun.

- Learn to reframe conflicts in your relationships as windows of opportunity. Refrain from judgment. Seek help from trusted friends or professionals when things get rocky. Get creative and explore other resources to help nurture your relationships and move through challenging times.

26

Betsy O'Reilly—The Resourceful Planner

Productivity is never an accident. It is always the result of a commitment to excellence, intelligent planning, and focused effort.

—Paul J. Meyer

A friend and I once facilitated a retreat titled "Healing of Memories." During the course of three days, everyone engaged in a variety of group and individual exercises, including storytelling. No surprise, the stories covered an array of harrowing topics that ranged from abuse and alcoholism to divorce and bankruptcy. At the end of the second day, the group came together for a glass of wine and an informal discussion, during which we encouraged questions and comments about the program content. After fielding a handful of remarks, I noticed an older woman named Iris sitting by herself. She wore a rather pensive expression, causing me to wonder if she might have something to say.

"Tell me, Iris, was there anything about the first two days that that resonated with your experience?" I asked.

She seemed uncomfortable with the question and took a moment to think before answering.

"Well, truthfully, I feel a little embarrassed," she finally replied. "I'm afraid I have nothing very dramatic or painful to add to what I've heard so far. My life has been blessedly calm and pretty predictable."

Her comments served as a good reminder that a Plan B can be blessedly calm and pretty predictable. In fact, frequently a Plan A doesn't implode but simply runs out of steam. Other times, a natural course of events, such as aging or a move to a different state or country, precipitates creation of a new blueprint. In any case, changing direction does not require a catastrophe. We assured Iris that her calm and predictable situation qualified as both gift and asset.

The same could be said about a Greenwich, Connecticut, woman whose journey also be could described as calm and predictable. Betsy O'Reilly had the right education and skills to launch her Plan A with confidence. Her approach to Plan B activated her calm and resourceful nature. She combined this with her desire to create a service that offered college students a gold mine of jobs, and employers a talent pool of top-job candidates. Her dream also required her willingness to make a change and the careful preparation that accompanied it.

It all started predictably enough. Betsy left school, ready for a career in the banking industry. She went to work at the Chicago Board of Trade, a plum job by any standards. Just about the time she got settled into the grueling hours and demanding work, Betsy encountered a major detour. This time it involved her husband's work.

"That first major shift took place when Ed accepted a job in Switzerland," Betsy explained. "I followed him overseas, a traditional role for a spouse, though I did find my own avenue to new work in Switzerland."

Though already experienced in the banking industry her new job involved shifting gears from trading to equity sales and marketing. Hence, Betsy stayed within her industry of choice but moved from an internally based trading role to a sales position. The work provided her with new opportunities and skill development that would serve her well later.

Eventually, Betsy and Ed moved from Zurich to London and started a family. After the birth of their second child, Betsy reached a tipping point that beckoned her to rethink the future. How might she combine family, passion, and skills into a fruitful strategy that everyone could live with? Eventually, Betsy and her husband moved back to the United States when her children were three and five years old.

"I realized I wanted to keep working well into my eighties," said Betsy. "It had become time to invest in myself and to create something substantial that I could do for years to come."

Even during her years in banking and equities, she always knew that a Plan B was going to be important, something to work toward. She also figured that her best guarantee for finding meaningful work was to create the job she really wanted. Her children were growing up and, at ages eight and ten, were busy with their own activities, prompting Betsy to pause and consider what made sense for the future. What could she manage? How could she best use her expertise while participating in the joys and needs of a growing family?

Ultimately, Betsy planned her own Plan B. It was not the result of a job loss or the house burning to the ground. It was the result of her internal questioning. She knew she wanted to make a difference, and she knew she wanted to make more impact than she could make in a corporate job. The challenge was to take time to develop a first-rate strategy.

The idea grew from her college experience of doing odd jobs. Though she always felt there was real value in those jobs, such work never made it into a résumé, nor was it even recognized as *real* work. Babysitting, piano lessons, tutoring— they all required dedication and effort yet never garnered much respect from future employers.

I too remember those jobs and tackled a few while attending the University of Wisconsin, Madison. I remember on Monday afternoons taking the bus to the suburbs to do a monster laundry and iron dress shirts for a busy family. At one point in my sophomore year, I had a job walking an old dog and preparing supper for a couple who came home each evening well fortified with martinis. Maybe it was their date night. Anyway, neither job provided me with a work history. As for the martini couple, they always seemed a little mystified to find me in their kitchen.

Driven to help college kids find an opportunity to work *and* build their work résumés, Betsy and two resourceful business partners, Bridie Clark Loverro and Andra Newman, created QuadJobs, an online job board linking employment-driven college kids with local families and businesses in need of good-quality help. All three women had once partaken in the odd-jobs syndrome and were convinced they had a much better idea.

They started recruiting students in August 2014 at Fairfield University; Norwalk Community College; Manhattanville College in Purchase, New York; Sacred Heart University at Fairfield; the State University of New York; and the University of Connecticut at Stamford. They also have been working with colleges to target small businesses such as Rotary Clubs, Kiwanis, and other organizations that might need extra hands to help with special events or e-mail campaigns.

Their focus on college and graduate students seemed like a natural choice. Flexibility of schedules and a variety of skills meant they could develop a deep pool of talent, everything from a clever math tutor to an accomplished painter, lawn mower, or furniture mover. Each student comes fully vetted and prepared to work. Each must land and complete his or her jobs, while their employers are encouraged to review their performance. QuadJobs tracks every job a student takes and gathers performance reviews from employers once the work is complete. They call this track record a student's JobGPA, and it becomes a valuable tool to help employers make informed hires.

"Were essentially taking the old-fashioned word-of-mouth networking idea and turning it into a digital format," explained Betsy. The employer feedback plays an essential role because it gives prospective employers a level of confidence in hiring a student from the QuadJobs program. At the same time, it gives a student an immediate work reference without having to make phone calls."

The service is free to students. Employers pay $8.95 per month for a subscription fee in exchange for the ability to post unlimited listings for full- or part-time, seasonal, or one-time jobs.

Betsy and her colleagues are confident that college students want to work—but differently than in the past. They can take jobs throughout the year, but they just can't commit to a schedule. Increased demands on all young people in and after school make it difficult for them to commit to ongoing work. They are, however, able to commit to intermittent jobs, and this is the niche QuadJobs intends to fill.

"Much has changed with kids," said Betsy. "I had time after school to get a job. Now, kids have so many extracurricular demands, nobody is doing the Saturday job anymore. And college-to-workforce has become so competitive that a young person had better get an internship that will impress a prospective employer."

Internships, however, have become more difficult to find and even harder to land. Further, she feels that many internships amount to little more than filling time or getting coffee for one's boss. Too often, these positions don't encourage students to think on their feet or problem solve, as they must with QuadJobs assignments.

"I am thrilled to be a cofounder and CEO of QuadJobs," said Betsy. "As business owners, we understand the need for flexible, smart help. We've relied on QuadJobs to get our own business off the ground and our school captains remain an integral part of our team as we grow. The students we've hired have consistently exceeded our expectations and added real value."

As a woman who knows the meaning of long hours and high expectations in financial markets and investment banking, Betsy O'Reilly has made a change. It was not an impulsive or uninvited change, but one that she approached in the same manner she approached her previous professional life—with thought, care, and a well-prepared strategy. She calls it her

Plan B. Her student talent pool most likely calls it a college employment dream.

Consider This: Nothing Beats a Solid Plan

One look at the daily newspaper or TV news would suggest that chaos surrounds us and mapping an even path to the future is impossible. Not true! Creating a Plan B often begins with clear thinking and steady preparation. Betsy O'Reilly provides a fine example of a great outcome that began with a great idea and a solid plan to back it up.

A move to a new home, a new job, or a new adventure prompted by children leaving for college provides the perfect occasion for us to organize our thoughts before taking a next step. Changing direction does not require pain or crisis. It might, however, require shifting our perceptions to see the hidden opportunities ahead.

Think of a time when you found yourself making a plan that was not driven by a setback or emergency. Describe the gifts or assets you brought to the planning table.

- Intuition?
- Research?
- Patience?
- Tenacity?
- Preparation?

What previously undiscovered or untested talents came to light during this process?

27

Return to Your Senses

I had the right to remain silent ... but I didn't have the ability.
—Ron White

Each of our seasons speaks from its own mystery. Each reveals messages about life's passages. In late October and November, the mood of fall changes. The days take on more subtle shades of still mornings and early darkness. The end of daylight saving time directs us toward beef stew, good books, and PBS reruns of *Foyle's War*. November is about becoming recharged for the next chapter. A look at my own garden reveals that maple trees have already set their buds for spring.

With this in mind, early morning last Thanksgiving, I pulled on warm clothes and set out for a walk with my dog, Winnie. We live in a neighborhood of 1950s bungalows, statuesque churches, and tree-lined campuses of Macalester College and the University of Saint Catherine. Giant oaks stand guard along the boulevards, and on this November day, their oak leaves still clung to the branches, braced against a sky that signaled a coming snowfall. Gray squirrels scampered through the dry leaves to rush up the half-naked English ivy climbing on the academic buildings. Highbush cranberries and naked lilac hedges framed an austere skyline.

Strolling through the leaves and deserted cul-de-sac, I observed the first glimmers of lamplight deep within a particularly handsome home. The neighborhood slowly began to awaken. Watching households emerge from the dawn filled me with a sensation of closeness to all those who stirred inside. I imagined them shuffling about in their bathrobes, feeding the cat, or sitting at the kitchen table with a hot cup of coffee. Some might have prayed, or worried, or simply read the morning newspaper. Within hours, their houses would overflow with the commotion of family and holiday guests. It all served as a reminder that there is life after November.

For centuries we lived in a sensuous world in which people relied on the ear and all the sense organs. Reality was experienced by sight, hearing, touch, smell, and taste. The oral story held a position of great importance to culture and history. An early morning November walk could be trusted to reveal important truths. Obviously, none of our senses disappeared with the introduction of science and technology, but today, the world about which they tell us has become suspect. If we can't come up with hard evidence on a particular topic and the metrics that prove its value, not many people are ready to believe it. The soulful experience remains dubious and lacking in credibility. In such a world, it's essential that we don't lose sight of personal reflection and the value of self-knowledge. These are not time-wasters but trustworthy sources of truth that help us safely navigate rough patches as well as fruitful outcomes. We learn that how we care is as important as what we know. We realize the folly of worshiping competency and in believing we must always be doing something that produces results. Ultimately, we learn never to become ashamed of the heart and all its implications of softness.

Some say today's quest to recover ancient healing traditions is a reaction to Descartes's world. Many of these traditions attempt to recover some of the vital acoustical senses amid our encounters with life. This is important because despite the value and contributions of Descartes's worldview, it defines life merely as what is material and observable. It defines life on very stingy terms.

So in the month when the earth and her inhabitants settle into violet stillness, perhaps it's life itself that waits for us to return to our senses.

Consider This: Earth, Our Island Home, as Source of Wisdom

All living creatures respond to the earth's seasonal transformations. Hibernating and migrating patterns, social and working patterns all demonstrate the influence of our earth recreating itself. We who know something about northern winters tend to believe the research that says people become more depressed during months when there are few hours of daylight. On the other hand, a Minnesota author might report that he gets more writing done during the dark and chilly months. Whether we're in our flannel pajamas by 7:00 p.m. or scraping the windshield of our car, winter alters our daily living patterns. In fact, all the seasons influence the way we live, what we wear, the foods we eat, and the homes we build. We respond in countless ways to the cycle of the seasons and the qualities of the earth.

Our interest in the earth is no accident or fleeting trend. We have a vital need to be close to the earth and to all her expressions. It is critical that we learn to protect and preserve her precious resources and fragile beauty. She is vulnerable as we are vulnerable. Even our vast resources of technology and science do not make us less vulnerable. We are born from the earth and nurtured by her, and we will ultimately return to her. We live on an island home in a vast expanse of interstellar space, galaxies, suns, and planets. We are assailable

"Listen," a fellow chaplain once said to me after a particularly tense meeting, "I hope that I've learned to never miss an opportunity to keep my mouth shut and hear what's really happening."

To listen is to hear, attend closely to, heed, give ear, and give audience. To listen requires silencing ourselves so as to create an empty space in which our thoughts and dreams can emerge or another person can feel safe expressing his or hers.

Listening lies at the heart of life flow. It also lies at the heart of justice, love, and peace. Our need to listen is surpassed only by our need to connect with one another and to the earth, our island home.

28

Artika Tyner—In Pursuit of Service

The meaning of life is to find your gift. The purpose of life is to give it away.

—Pablo Picasso

Artika Tyner, EdD, invites the above quote into her life every day. Educator, lawyer, author, and advocate for justice, Artika teaches and models public policy and leadership at the University of Saint Thomas in Saint Paul, Minnesota. She also trains graduate students and countless others on how to become social engineers, capable of carving new inroads to justice and freedom. I met Artika on Martin Luther King Jr. Day. It was a day to reflect on the progress and perils of social justice and the meaning of servant leadership in America.

If I thought Artika's job seemed a formidable task, I quickly learned that it was just one of her Herculean commitments to service. It also shapes the life plan she has pursued for as long as she can remember.

"My foremothers were domestics," she explained. "They migrated to Minnesota from the South. I was the first to interrupt that history by gaining a college education. I was always interested in what my grandmother Nellie Lightfoot did with her hands, but she always encouraged me to read and work with my mind instead."

To a certain degree, Artika's family expected her to be the first family member to go to college. Neither her grandmother nor her mother, Jacklyn Milton, could provide much disposable income, but both made certain she had the necessary books and transportation to get to school activities.

"My mother always told me to pick up the mantle of leadership through education," said Artika. "Mom never let adversity stop her from reaching for the stars, and she taught me the same. I started to see that education was a necessary tool. For me, it has been the tool that enables me to understand and contribute to the world of peace and justice." It also has been the tool that guided me toward law school and becoming a civil rights lawyer."

Artika has never gone looking for her Plan A. Instead, she believes the plan found her. She instinctively knew that each piece of education she added to her cache would help. Her intuition told her that all this work developed character and skills. It also taught her the language of power—as in, power to bring change. Hence, her thirst for education has propelled her beyond law school to a master's of public policy and leadership degree and a doctorate in leadership.

A lifetime Minnesota resident, Artika grew up in Saint Paul's historic Rondo neighborhood, named after an early settler, Joseph Rondeau. By the 1950s, about 85 percent of Saint Paul's African American population lived in this old neighborhood that was divided into diverse cultural sections, such as Oatmeal Hill and Cornmeal Valley.

"I'm the youngest of three, raised by a single mom," Artika said. "She ran a home daycare center for twenty years. She always embraced a sense of purpose that spelled service."

Artika received her first education scholarship award in 1999 from the Page Education Foundation. She's hardly stopped for air since then. "The foundation ignited my passion for service in the community and guided me on my journey to becoming a lawyer," she explained.

Founded by Minnesota Supreme Court justice and NFL Hall of Famer Alan Page, the foundation exemplifies Alan's deep and abiding belief in the importance of education. Recognizing a need for our education system to reach more young people of color, he used his 1988 induction into the NFL Hall of Fame to launch the Page Education Foundation with his wife, Diane. From its inception, the foundation has offered money and encouragement to students of color who face barriers to attaining their educational dreams. In exchange for financial aid, Page scholars must also mentor school-aged children. It was an organization that suited Artika to a T.

"Everyone has the ability, opportunity, and obligation to make this world a better place," stated Justice Page. "When we help others, we can ensure educational opportunities, improve our character, and begin to address the problems of race. All we have to do is act, and act we must. Artika embodies the mission of the Page Education Foundation through her commitment to education and service."

Upon completing the first leg of her scholarly journey, a bachelor's degree in education, Artika was on track for a career teaching high school English. However, once she began student teaching, she discovered the enormous disparities among her students—disparities in vocabulary, food, health, access to education, and housing. The opportunity gap between children from affluent circumstances and children from poor ones shocked her.

"That was my aha moment that pointed me toward law school," said Artika. "I realized, yes, I could teach, but I could do more." Law offered a language of power and a platform from which to impact a larger audience.

Then came the next chapter, a master's in public policy and leadership in order to gain tools to effect social change through policy reform efforts. Later, inspired by the legacy of W. E. B. Du Bois, Artika obtained a doctorate in leadership. These scholarly achievements added up to far more than degrees to hang on her office wall. They gave her a foundation from which she could make a real difference in facilitating social justice.

It's safe to say that Artika's interest in law reaches well beyond what happens on the bench. She describes the law as having the capacity to create change and open access to human rights. Her new book, *The Lawyer as Leader*, develops a vision of lawyers not as corporate suits but as servant leaders. She sees law as a healing profession. Her book presents a road map that helps lawyers see themselves as transformative leaders promoting social change.

Artika teaches and models a vision of lawyering compatible with the principles of restorative justice. Restorative justice provides a framework for conceptualizing justice, based on positive values and principles. It enlarges the scope of justice by including the needs and roles of offenders as well as victims and communities.

"The social justice challenges of our time are enormous," said Artika. "About one in seven US residents lives in poverty, and the disparity between the haves and the have-nots is wider than at any point since the Great Depression. The poor are largely marginalized from the public-policy process and often are unable to assert their legal rights in regard to basic necessities, such as nutrition, health, shelter, income, education, and protection from violent physical abuse."

She described a social justice lawyer as one who recognizes his or her capacity to make change for the benefit of vulnerable others who have less power and access and then works to make those changes.

So what does restorative justice in our communities look like from a practical standpoint? "It might mean we go back to American history to look at the facts surrounding racial justice and civil rights," explained Artika. "Borrowing from the model of truth and reconciliation commissions, we might offer an open forum or talking circles, where people can grapple with these issues. At the micro-level, it might pertain to a workplace conflict or family conflict. How do you bring people together to talk about community-building?"

Artika taught law from 2006 to 2014. During that time she also codeveloped a curriculum for the Community Justice Project, composed of law students engaged in research, education, and mobilization around such issues as racial disparities, gang violence, and relationships with police.

Currently, she teaches a master's-level class in leadership and public policy at the University of Saint Thomas School of Education.

"I'm working with leaders from school boards, police departments, education, and many different walks of life," she said. "I've expanded my net beyond lawyers."

Not only does Artika believe that education moves beyond the four walls of institutions, she is living proof of this. When I asked if she had encountered many roadblocks and challenges along the way, she replied, "Not really." But if she did find herself in one of those tough spaces, she would remember her ninety-year-old great-aunt Geneva Kirtley, who still lives independently in Chicago.

"She personified leadership early in her life and mine. As a young adult, she helped our family migrate from sharecropping in Mobile, Alabama, to the North."

Whether inspired by her daughter or just plain inspired, Artika's mother launched her own higher education plan. Jacklyn earned her bachelor's degree while Artika earned her law degree. Then in 2012, Jacklyn received her master's in education as her daughter completed her doctorate.

"We enjoyed duel celebrations that year," Artika declared.

Jacklyn works **for** Amherst H. Wilder Foundation, a nonprofit social services organization that provides research and community initiatives that address the needs of vulnerable people in Saint Paul and beyond.

To what or to whom does Artika credit her considerable accomplishments? She would tell you it has been a combination of her upbringing and her Christian faith.

"If we are going to be part of a global community, we need to be facilitators," she offered. "I always used to tease my mother by saying I'm a citizen of the world. I had the best experience learning about other cultures." Her mother answered by modeling education as a tool for engagement and working in the community for improved quality of life.

Today, Artika is busy building a social-change movement by reimagining education and reimagining the very essence of leadership. Her work is inspiring people across the globe to unleash the transformative power within their hands.

"I'm confident that we can move beyond race, tribe, and creed to our shared humanity and shared destiny," she declared. "We are all interconnected."

Consider This: Practice the Art of Serving Others

Finding harmony in our lives through serving others begins with a desire and a capacity to listen. Listen to your heart speak to you about its own loss and need; listen to those you love. Listening fosters healing and informs our approach to service. Listening also helps us

- discover where we are and where we want to be on our life's path.
- identify our passion and vision for the future.
- see what pains us or inhibits our moving forward with new plans.
- shine a light on our next steps.
- discover our deepest yearnings.

29

Noah's Notes—Are We Disappearing with Age?

Madam stopped in today to talk about our winter foray up North on the Gunflint Trail. Since food preparation is always top of mind for this annual snow event, I figured she wanted to discuss menus and my recent Pillsbury Bake-Off winner. But I was wrong. She surprised me by opening our coffee klatch with a highly unusual revelation.

"I'm invisible," she declared, while pulling off her chopper's mitts and flumping on my horsehair lounger. "Obviously, I have reached a final plan in life when I could be carrying a pipe bomb under one arm, and a TSA agent wouldn't even bother to ask me to take my shoes off."

"So if you're invisible, why can I see you nibbling on one of my freshly baked Nickerdoodles?" I inquired. "And by the way, you are wearing Dickie coveralls and an earflap hat, aren't you? That makes you pretty visible in a crowd, if you ask me."

She sighed deeply, eying me as if I had grown a moustache. "Yes, Noah, but you're missing the point," she persisted. "I feel like as though I've become beige, nothing more than a vanishing puff of Glade air freshener. Even the dog has started to look at me as if we've never met. Why, just yesterday I took her to a play date, and afterward, she ran right past me and jumped into Ellie Amundson's minivan."

"Well, we both know that she's fond of the Amundsons' elderly Westie, Ned," I offered, though immediately regretted calling Ned elderly.

Then I remembered reading on Wikipedia that humans start to shrink when they hit a certain age. Come to think of it, Madam did mention that her doctor said she'd lost an inch of altitude over the last few years. But for Pete's sake, she's still five foot eight, which seems visible enough to get by.

Suffice it to say our Gunflint Trail planning meeting would have to wait. Instead, I assumed my life-coach position and delicately asked Madam a few questions, beginning with, "What was your first clue that you had become hardly noticeable?"

She pondered that for a moment. "It all started when the Costco checkout clerk handed me my grocery receipt and said, 'Thank you, sir.'"

"Um ... do you think it had anything to do with that earflap hat you seem to be living in these days? Or perhaps Costco clerks don't know many mature females who dress in coveralls and wear spurs."

After holding forth about the countless horsewomen she knew who grocery shopped and lunched at Panera Bread with their spurs on, she asked what I meant by *mature* females. This took me a moment.

"Then there was the hostess at Amy Lou's House of Pancakes," she declared. "This woman could clearly see that I was next in line, yet she tossed the guy behind me a radiant smile and hauled him off to a table next to a sunny window with a view. Or how about last week, when my postal carrier handed me an audit notification from the IRS addressed to Mr. M. Farr, Esquire?"

"Well, I suppose one could look at that as better news for you than for Mr. Farr," I added encouragingly.

She was on a role. "Monday morning, Jake's Tru Test Glass delivered my new shower door to the Delrose family next door," she pressed on. "And two of my clients forgot to pay me, probably because they forgot my name. Why, just last night, a friend and I went to see *Fifty Shades of Grey*, and the guy at the window sold me a children's ticket."

I resisted the temptation to ask how she liked the movie.

At first Madam's fussing struck me as a "tempest in a teapot," as they say. But suddenly, all this business of vanishing started to get to me. I found myself wrestling with worrisome questions. Could she be right? If so, was she describing an aging problem or a wardrobe problem? Could she be facing the first step in life's next chapter, or was this just a tipoff to hire a personal shopper? In any case, I also realized that I too am a bit long in the tooth and underwhelming in the wardrobe department. So I figured it was high time to get myself in front of a mirror and make sure that I haven't disappeared.

And another thing, I concluded it was high time we both started wearing more red.

Consider This: Life at Any Age Is an Event Worth Showing Up For

At some point along the way, I began to realize that life is not just a journey toward old age. It's also a turning point at which we can choose to keep growing and enjoying new experiences or vanish into a closet, where we keep making smaller choices. This does not mean taking up hot yoga. Nor does it demand running a marathon or taking up kickboxing. It does suggest that we working at saying yes—it's much more interesting than hunkering down with a resounding no.

- When a friend asks you to join her for a movie tonight, and you don't feel like driving in the city after dark, ask your friend to pick you up, or ask a family member to drop you off at the theater.

- When your hair stylist says, "Do you want the usual cut or color today?" how about replying, "Let's try something new"?

- If your cousin suggests bowling on Sunday afternoon at the Medina Entertainment Center, and you haven't bowled since high school, remember how much fun it was then, and accept the invitation.

- Just keep in mind, saying yes offers a far better return on investment than saying no.

30

Nettie Rosenow—Sometimes a Plan Finds Us

Flow—a state of heightened focus in which a person is completely immersed with intense and creative engagement in an activity such as art, play or work.
> —Mihaly Csikszentmihalyi,
> positive psychologist

Years ago when my mother tried to convince me to practice the piano, she faced a daunting hurdle—my horse. According to her, I suffered from amnesia every time I went to the barn. I forgot to come home for lunch. I missed dinner and, of course, I failed to keep my lesson appointment with my piano teacher, Mrs. Rogness. Decades later my friend Nettie and I went to her barn to fool around with a couple of her Quarter Horse fillies. Hours later, Nettie's husband, John, showed up at the gate to ask if we planned to have supper any time soon. It was getting dark, though neither of us noticed the sun had gone down.

Some would call this thoughtless, irresponsible behavior. Positive psychologist Mihaly Csikszentmihalyi would likely call it "flow," or the loss of time and self-consciousness that occur when we are completely absorbed in an activity. A growing body of scientific evidence suggests that flow is highly correlated with happiness.[7]

---

[7] ted.com/speakers/mihaly_csikszentmihalyi

Much as we would love to make "flow" the main event in our day-to-day experience, the hobbies, passions, and creative goals that light our fires often take a backseat to primary plans. Such was the case with my friend Nettie Rosenow. The test for her—and for each of us who gives up something precious in exchange for personal and professional obligations—is how do we preserve the precious part? In Nettie's case, she put aside what she held closest to her heart— her horses. But she made certain they didn't get lost in the fray of building a dairy business with her classmate and future husband, John.

"My whole life, for as long as I can remember, has been dominated by my interest in horses," said Nettie. "I bought my own horse, a yearling paint filly named June Bug, when I was only thirteen. She cost thirty-five dollars."

Now, fifty years later, Nettie has never been without a horse. Yet maintaining her dream hasn't been easy. As a young woman, she packed her suitcase, loaded June Bug in the trailer, and headed off to college with plans of becoming a veterinarian. It wasn't long before that plan changed and life took a sharp turn in an unexpected direction. That was when she met John, a fifth-generation Wisconsin dairy farmer. Eventually, Nettie changed her major to animal science. She graduated with honors and headed down a new path, never having envisioned life as a partner in the dairy business. It looked as if her Plan A had chosen her.

"I remember John's cousin asking us why we were going to farm and not use our education," said Nettie. "Truthfully, education stimulated my inquisitive mind, but it became outdated fairly quickly. Technology in agriculture soon exploded, and if we hoped to succeed in the dairy business, we had to keep up. But the habit of lifelong learning has expanded my interests in so many directions."

Her partnership with John in the dairy business and eventually the compost business has grown into a long and successful one, though not without setbacks. One pivotal event—a fire that destroyed their dairy barn and half their herd—nearly sent her down a separate path, training horses for the public. John too was quite capable of making a career change, running a different business or seeking employment in a new field. Instead, they agreed to go forward together. John's younger brother joined the partnership, and they build a new modern barn and parlor, bought cows, and worked very hard for many years. Later, they joined with a neighbor and doubled their facilities and cow numbers. The horses had to take a backseat but remained a placeholder for the future.

Over the years, Nettie and John have enjoyed the rewards of becoming responsible leaders, changing the face of dairy business models. John's opinions are valued on numerous boards, and he appreciates the respect of his peers and his tenure as past president of the Wisconsin Milk Board. An environmentally informed farmer, he has built a thriving compost business as an outgrowth of their dairy cattle waste.

As animal lovers who depend on cattle for a living, the Rosenows care for their cows humanely, enabling them to produce and reproduce in good health. They teach all their employees to treat the cows humanely as well. Their herd of a thousand head of cows and calves requires watchful care twenty-four hours a day. Like a village of a thousand people, someone is always sick. Both Nettie and John put in long hours with limited vacations.

"The genetics program is my job," explained Nettie. "I breed the cows, and breeding better cows is something that takes a lifetime to perfect."

Like the advancement of technology, the right kind of cow has changed and improved over the years. Valuable DNA information makes it possible to select bulls for superior production and type. Nettie's balanced approach to their breeding program has produced healthy cows that also are superior in production and type.

"I'm proud of the progress we've made," she acknowledged. "Nearly all of our cows are registered Holsteins, which gives us records that help us improve the entire breed."

Though she has sometimes struggled as a woman working in agriculture, Nettie has enjoyed real success with changing stereotypes within the field. Equally rewarding, she's been able to refocus on her first love, her horses. Years of study and engagement with top professionals have given her the skills to train and breed her own fine mares.

"I've bought better horses through the years and have some I'm really proud of," she said. Her American Quarter Horse mares carry exceptional bloodlines, of horses such as Docs Hickory, Smart Little Lena, and High Brow Cat. Her breeding program continues to grow, as each year her mares produce a new crop of high-level–performance foals.

Nettie and John's decision to rebuild after their devastating fire grew from their desire to remain on the unspoiled land that John's family has owned for generations. Located in west central Wisconsin, an eagle's flight from the historic river town of Alma, the Rosenows' dairy sits in a valley just east of the steep Mississippi River bluffs. Their little slice of beauty must have looked like heaven to the Swiss and German immigrants who settled among the green valleys, hardwood forests, trout streams, and white-tailed deer.

"John's father, grandfather, and great-grandfather worked the same land," said Nettie. "It meant a great deal to them and to us. It gives us a real sense of place."

The landscape remains a constant that anchors them there. As a friend and frequent houseguest, I can confirm that the view out their kitchen window never gets old. Nettie rides her horses over the grassy hills. She and John walk together in the hay fields with their dog, Pepin. They know what it means to be married to the land.

"It's always a new experience, even though we've been on these paths and through these fields many, many times. It's not so much a feeling that the land is ours but that it's a privilege to live here," she offered.

So a few years ago, when she and John learned that their neighbors had leased fourteen hundred acres with the intention of mining frack sand, they were crushed. They found it hard to imagine how someone could place so little value on the land and create such conflict among their neighbors. Yet this fourteen-hundred-acre surprise marked only the beginning of the Buffalo County mining challenge. Before long, land developers and mining companies moved through the area, offering enticing monetary rewards and the promise of new jobs. Many landowners agreed to sell or cooperate with the growing frack sand movement. Others refused. Tensions grew throughout the valley and across the tiny agricultural communities.

As an intelligent woman determined to head off ruination of her home and livelihood, Nettie found her way to the county board. Or perhaps the county board found her. In any case, she was elected Buffalo County Supervisor and now chairs a zoning committee. She has hired a conservationist and has shifted reclamation of nonmetallic mines to the conservation department. The board also addresses concerns over the proliferation of mining applications and has written an amendment to protect the Great River Road in Buffalo County from over-industrialization.

Nettie never expected to step into the world of politics. But then, she never expected to spend all these years in the dairy business. Nor might she have expected preserving her dream of breeding and training great horses. Yet that inquisitive mind of hers persists. She continues to study the landscape and the environmental concerns surrounding mining and over-industrialization. She's become more comfortable speaking in public, expressing her opinions. Meanwhile, she still works hard at perfecting her breeding programs and can't wait for next year's colt crop.

"I really see this area as unique, beautiful, and worthy of our effort to save it," she concluded. "I hope that all our work to protect this place continues after we are gone. I hope others are motivated to do the same, to realize that the things we take for granted can be altered beyond recognition in the blink of an eye."

Consider This: When a Plan Picks You

Many years working in the field of health care has made one thing clear: health care chose me. I never planned to practice medicine or to work anywhere within a patient-care system, though opportunities kept showing up. Frankly, my interests leaned toward writing and art. Then, following high school graduation, I received a grant from the National Science Foundation to produce medical illustrations for a local hospital pathology laboratory. Next came a summer job as an aide, wheeling patients to therapy. Eventually, I began to work in the hospital communications department, writing and publishing patient education materials. This led to marketing and business development. And finally, my choice to pursue pastoral ministry placed me in a position of direct patient care, plus teaching medical residents how to communicate with families of very sick kids. The point is, I might not have chosen health care, but I ultimately developed a set of health and wellness skills that have served me well.

The same can be said for Nettie Rosenow. She "accidently" found herself in the dairy business, learning bovine genetics, nutrition, and health and now occupies a county board leadership position aimed at protecting the land and its natural resources. She might not have chosen this plan, but she is well suited for it.

The question is this: are we ready to release limiting beliefs to unlock our potential, even if this takes us in a direction we had not anticipated?

Consider a time when you accepted a task or role for which you initially felt ill suited but then turned out to be a valuable experience.

Think of a time when you were able to transform unpredictable events or even a bad job into a creative opportunity.

31

Look at Success from a Different Angle

Try not to become a man of success, but rather try to become a man of value.
—Albert Einstein

Once, out of the blue, I received an invitation to write a speech for a popular political figure. The address was to be given at an elegant dinner hosted by a local hospital foundation to honor the politician's personal physician for his years of service. I accepted the writing assignment with more curiosity than interest ... at least until I placed the first phone call to a colleague of the honoree.

"He's the finest doctor I've ever known," the fellow internist reported simply. "He's the kind of role model every physician could use."

A second call produced a comparable response: "His life gives meaning to qualities like humanness, patience, and compassion," the family friend related. "He deals with humble people as if they were important people and communicates sincerely with everyone he touches. And he never limits himself in his relationships."

After several more calls, I realized that the emerging portrait contained nothing about the man's clinical skills as a physician. While everyone with whom I spoke contributed some helpful and defining brushstroke, the observations and personal encounters had less to do with the doctor's professional achievements than with his character. But the award, as I understood it, was intended to honor his medical career. And of course, it did. In fact, this man's career had opened him to a dimension of spirit that everyone recognized as healing. They also recognized it as success.

Aside from his obvious kindness toward his patients, he seemed to inspire others in ways that helped them be well. His commitment to serve the life and people around him also strengthened the life within him and within his family. Though everyone insisted that he was a gifted physician, he had never let his professional training or clinical expertise remove any aspects of wholeness from him. He had never allowed any conditions of the health care business world to erode his relationships or negatively alter his call to serve others through medicine.

Years earlier, this physician decided to let go of the typical clinical obsession with fascinating medical problems, and instead immersed himself in the daily routine of a healer. With compassion and awe, he attended to both the bodies and souls of his patients. He found that a patient's spirit was not just a human potential but a human need, and he learned that too much scientific objectivity can cause one to miss the whole picture of health and healing. Though his clinical skills rewarded him with a respected practice, he never lost sight of who he was and what he wished to share with the world. He seemed destined to care for others, to seek wholeness, and to recognize the value and dignity of each person he touched.

At the award ceremony, several eminent guests regaled the audience with glowing stories about the honored guest, showering him with well-deserved accolades. Finally, the time for presentations arrived, and the physician shyly approached the microphone to make his acceptance speech. It was brief but, according to him, not brief enough.

"There is nothing that becomes a person more than silence," he began. "Silence is a safeguard for wisdom." Thus, with a simple and gracious thank-you, he returned to his seat.

If anybody was disappointed at his lack of ceremony, they never showed it. Everyone seemed to understand perfectly.

In a place of quiet wisdom, this man had developed an uncanny ability to nourish and strengthen people. He practiced a rare kind of medicine. His listening ear and hospitable heart clearly informed his clinical competence. He embraced a simplicity that was synonymous with humility—a word derived from the Latin word *humus,* or earth. To be humble means to be in touch with the earth and all her inhabitants.

We live in uprooted times and plenty of noise. It's so easy to inadvertently miss the wisdom of the heart. Some have even said that cardiac bypass surgery is a metaphor for our contemporary culture—a culture that has bypassed the heart. However, alienation and cynicism have no role in the fundamental truth that we need to connect with one another in sickness and in health. We must sustain ourselves and our own dreams but also those of others and of the larger community. Whether we're healing professionals or simply trying to find the path toward the next stage, we all gain life when we realize that mystery sustains much longer than does mastery.

Each of us is on a personal journey that offers limitless possibilities. Whether we teach school, care for children, or run for political office, nobody and nothing can take away our choice of how we will respond to those healing encounters. A physician faces a woman newly diagnosed with breast cancer. That physician steps outside his clinical space, removes the curtain that protects his heart, and listens. A friend makes room in her busy day for another whose dreams have met limitation and failure head-on. She touches the friend's hand and knows. A drug addict finds freedom in recovery. A nurse places a cool cloth on the forehead of a fifteen-year-old girl who has just miscarried her baby. Sometimes a smile, touch, or kind presence requires nothing more than silence to perform its work.

If the honored physician I've described brought just a single quality to his practice, it was his gift of attentive silence that had everything to do with his genuine engagement.

32

Noah's Notes—When to Say No to a Plan B in Horticulture

I never felt moved to garden. A weekly CSA (Community Supported Agriculture) delivery full of carrots makes a delicious gift, but last year, when I was craving a fresh rhubarb crisp, our CSA farmer Clyde Gunderson delivered a bushel of kale. Incidentally, green kale combined with blueberries and a shot of apple juice makes another color: brown. Hence, the term Poo Smoothie made its way into our food lexicon. But more to the point, why squander good money on fertilizer and compost when Andres and I toss it out of my room every day?

Madam, on the other hand, swoons when the spring seed catalogs arrive. Daffodils, mums, heirloom tomatoes—she sticks them in the ground the minute she can chisel a hole in the dirt. A case in point: last spring, she expanded her petite kitchen garden into an enterprise worthy of the University of Minnesota's Landscape Arboretum. Size, by the way, didn't necessarily spell success. Just about the time she popped a fabulous-looking head of cauliflower into boiling water, an entire worm family swam for cover. Thus ended the blanch-and-freeze operation. Yet Madam is nothing if not persistent.

Armed with this information, I should not have been surprised when she texted me to ask if I would bring big Sven over to her place to help tidy up last year's botanical behemoth. According to her, it was a job requiring horsepower from manly specimens like the two of us.

"We'll need to pull your Comfy Sundowner trailer out of the shed for this little undertaking," she added. "All the garden litter and leftover pumpkins will never fit in the Subaru Outback."

"Um, how about bagging the stuff and leaving it on the curb for Aspen Waste Management?" I suggested. If memory serves, last year's cleanup produced a number of hidden surprises, including slippery night crawlers and a petrified vole.

I tried to explain. "The idea of thawing rabbit poo and rotted hostas joyriding in my Comfy Sundowner just feels wrong," I offered politely. "And sharing space with rodent carcasses doesn't appeal to Sven either. He might be a big shire, but he happens to be afraid of mice."

It helped her case that she kept referring to Sven and me as manly specimens. So with minimal coaxing and the promise of a Dairy Queen Moo Latte, we agreed to help. Sven loaded up our Bobcat Gator and a few pitchforks, and Madam drove us to her home for a morning of garden prep.

Once we filled the Comfy Sundowner, she announced, "Okay, boys, jump in. We're off to the Saint Claire Avenue compost site to get rid of this stuff."

We climbed in. Sven tied a dishtowel over his nose, cowboy style, to protect against the Eau de Squirrel fragrance that wafted from within. Fortunately, the ride took just minutes, though lots of other folks had the same idea. Fully loaded cars and trucks wound around the driveway and down the street. So we caught a quick nap while we waited. Once Madam reached the front of the line, she pulled up to the nearest pile of organic matter and started pitching, while Sven and I waited inside the trailer.

Folks must have been feeling jumpy with all that waiting because soon enough, a fracas broke out somewhere in the next row over.

"What's all that shouting?" whispered Sven.

I stretched my neck, attempting to get a look out my window, just in time for a rotten tomato to smack the glass. I ducked, and Sven gasped. More shouts followed. "It's coming from that red van," I whispered back. "Can you see anything from your side?"

"All I can see is Madam pointing at a sign that says *No Guns, Fighting, or Foul Language Allowed on These Premises. Violators Will Be Prosecuted*!" Just about then, a muddy cantaloupe ricocheted off the trailer door as Madam yanked it open and jumped in. Armed with a pitchfork and a plastic bag, she appeared ready for a firm discussion.

"Why don't you just call 911 and let the authorities stop over for a word," I suggested to no avail (no pun intended).

"You boys don't move a whisker," she commanded, disregarding my entreaty. "I'm tossing the rest of this stuff right out the back door, and we'll be out of here in a flash. "

By now, the shouting had escalated to an unruly level, and I could see the site supervisor galloping across the parking area, waving his fist. A woman in a pink tube top bellowed at her boyfriend, Frank, calling him a good-for-nothing lump. A guy named Billy threw a punch at a fellow driving a Ford Super Duty pickup. Just at that moment, a can of beer made it through the pickup driver's open window. That was when the foul language struck a high note.

Meanwhile, Madam kept pushing garden remains out the trailer door. She then slammed and bolted the tailgate, jumped in her Dodge Ram, and drove for home like a volunteer firefighter on her way to a four-alarmer.

"What the heck was that about?" Sven squeaked as we bounced over a curb and up the hill. "I thought compost sites were friendly places where folks traded tips on grilling sweet corn."

"Hmm ... I suppose that sign should have been our first clue," I reasoned out loud. "I'll have to admit, though, that woman in pink had quite an arm to pitch a full can of beer through a truck window."

Sven shuddered at the thought. "Yes, but do you think this will keep Madam from gardening this year?" he croaked, wincing at the prospect of getting beaned by a can of Summit Pale Ale.

"Not a chance," I replied. "Once she gets a big idea, she's hard to deter."

33

Practice Personal Courage

You gain strength, courage, and confidence by every experience in which you really stop to look fear in the face. You are able to say to yourself, "I lived through this horror. I can take the next thing that comes along."
—Eleanor Roosevelt

A month or so after New York City endured the blow of commercial aircraft, breaking her heart, I heard a curious story on National Public Radio. The author of the story had been in Brooklyn on that fateful day of September 11 and happened upon a neighborhood park shortly after the first plane hit the World Trade Center. People were congregating in the park, gazing in disbelief at the smoldering skyline of downtown Manhattan. Clutched in twos and threes, they hunkered around their portable radios, incredulous over the emerging details of what they were witnessing. With morning coffee still cooling in their cups and leashed dogs straining to meet their unfamiliar canine neighbors, each of the observers struggled to grasp the significance of the event they watched unfolding at a distance.

After observing the worried clutch for some time, the author noticed a single individual at the far edge of the park. Unlike the others, the man had no coffee or family pet at his side, only a set of golf clubs and a large bucket of balls. With a seven iron in hand, he methodically placed one ball after another in front of him. Carefully arranging his feet and correcting his grip, he addressed each ball and hit it out of the park into a snarl of weeds. He showed no interest in retrieving the balls, nor did he look up at the blazing concrete skyline crumbling before him. The author watched with wonder at this fellow who seemed so indifferent about the mounting catastrophe. Torn between his desire to learn the answer and his unease about prying into a stranger's privacy, he finally got out of his car and approached the golfer.

"Good morning," he offered quietly, so as not to startle the stranger. "Excuse me, but do you know what has taken place at the World Trade Center?" The man did not reply. "Do you often come to this park to hit balls?" the author queried tentatively. Again, he got no response.

After one more prolonged stretch of silence, the golfer looked up, not at the skyline but at the author.

"Yes, I do know what has taken place," he replied evenly. Then he addressed yet another ball and drove it into the tall grass. "I know what I've heard. I don't understand it, and I can't do anything about it. But I can hit these golf balls."

Hearing this story, I remembered going to visit a couple whose teenage son, Jacob, had been struck and killed by a drunk driver. Once a promising athlete, the boy underwent a football-career–ending knee injury in his junior year of high school. While many might parents anticipated a bitter response to his dashed hopes of becoming a star quarterback, Jacob steered his adolescent vigor into becoming a fine musician and gifted photographer. Responsible, mature, and beloved by his classmates, he was peddling his bike to a job one afternoon when a man with numerous alcohol-related driving citations careened off the road and killed him.

Upon arriving at Jacob's home on the morning of the funeral, I met friends and relatives bustling about, preparing food and greeting guests. His father, Drew, a fireman uncomfortable in his black suit, was doing his best to shepherd their younger children off to church. When I asked after his wife, Karla, he pointed me to the backyard, where I found her disheveled in her nightgown, barefoot, weeding the garden.

With a garbage bag in one hand, she worked her way up and down the rows of onions and radishes, removing every piece of alien foliage and placing it in the bag. Finally, I asked her how she was getting along. She responded in much the same manner as the golfer.

"I can't make sense of my child's death. I don't know what the future holds, but I need to clean up this garden."

I have always trusted people when they say these kinds of things. Karla really did need to clean up her garden. In fact, a need to manage something, even something small, becomes a critical piece in restoring order and preparing for a new and different journey.

In the Hebrew Bible, the book of Ecclesiastes is called Qoheleth. It was this wisdom figure, Qoheleth, whose purpose was not so much to teach about God but rather to tell what he had discovered about life—what humans might gain from life. He sets forth certain viewpoints on the value of life. He outlines a doctrine of opposites, like two currents flowing between the same banks. Woven into the fabric of his composition, Qoheleth asks a larger question about the worth of life. What real value does life have to offer? How do we come to grips with the mystery and darkness of life, those shadowy parts we can't fix but can only walk through? Qoheleth confronts questions that have endured throughout human history, questions asked by the golfer, the mother, the unemployed husband, or the disillusioned divorcee. And we don't need to lose a child or witness the shattering of a city to step into that same field of reluctance.

The golfer's story happened on September 11. Later that fall I was driving back to Minnesota from visiting family and friends. The fields stood naked of their grains, and farm tractors bumped alongside roadsides, hauling corn and soybeans. The country stood quiet, waiting for the leaves to complete their cycle and become host to winter's softness and the hope for spring.

Hope or expectation serves a key ingredient in becoming whole. Hope provides purpose, direction, and a reason for being. It encourages a sense that we can transcend the present situation and reenter the flow of life. Hope is an attitude toward life, not just an occasional feeling we turn to when we need it. It is a disposition that says the future is an open one, and you or I can dare to believe it holds integrity and promise. That promise can occur even in the face of a loss or unforeseen detour. Hope ignites our capacity to see ourselves in a larger landscape, one in which we can cross over a hurdle into a future not yet defined.

Though I have no way of knowing whether the golfer in the public radio story moved forward into a current of hope, I suspect that his first steps were to reestablish some order to his psyche in the face of that day's events. His approach might not have been a conventional one, but managing his golf swing and basket of balls made perfect sense to him. From that point, I suspect that he continued to try to understand, to ask why, and hopefully, to move on to other healing measures. I was hopeful that he had family and trusted friends with whom he could express his grief and share simple pastimes. I also trust that he eventually settled into familiar routines that offered him pleasure and nourishment.

I do know something about the family whose son, Jacob, died. Once they muddled through the anguishing first months, Karla became a passionate advocate for Mothers Against Drunk Drivers (MADD). She then returned to her nursing career to share her gifts of compassion and clinical skill with other families. Drew resumed his work as a firefighter, never doubting for a minute that he had made good life choices in everything from his mate to his career. They found strength in their faith community, reconnected with old friends, and immersed themselves in their remaining children's activities. They bought the farm they had always dreamed of and today surround themselves with cherished grandchildren, ponies, exotic chickens, and an array of family pets. My guess is that each day they think of Jacob, and each day they see a reason for living.

Through the years I've listened to families and friends worry out loud about a future they cannot see. I too have wrung my hands over unseen and improbable events, as if my fretfulness might somehow stave off future disaster. I too have awakened in a fit of midnight insanity, convinced that I would never find another job to support myself or would be forced to spend my "retirement" years working crossword puzzles and talking to my goldfish. But I also know that when I get caught up in cynicism and worry, I neglect to fully live the path I'm already walking.

Each of us longs for balance and meaning in our lives. No matter if we are challenged by illness or thrilled to begin a new life with someone we love, meaning relates directly to our understanding of our life's purpose. Nurturing our souls involves creating a safe space in which we can move toward completeness, no matter where or how we choose to begin the journey. Lighting up our soul involves a personal conversation focused on well-being. When we have an opportunity to be heard and explore the meaning our experiences, we enlarge ourselves and reach beyond whatever we left behind. Nurturing souls expect reconciliation with what has happened and look forward to what lies ahead. While *wishing* desires specific things, *hoping* points to a belief in future promise, though not in details we can see or know.

We're not done yet. Creation continues. How we live life matters. Becoming our authentic selves also matters. We simply cannot know whom we will touch or be touched by along the way. We know it can be excruciatingly painful as well as breathtakingly beautiful. We belong to creation. The real question for each of us is not whether there is life after death but whether there is life after birth. Do we recognize it emerging from the dying and rising of each transition and daily challenge?

In every age there are people who feel abandoned by God and the universe. In each of our lives there are moments when we feel cut off from hope and love. Yet we must live in the real world of human paradox. It's a place where we won't be saved by the human condition, but we can grow and flourish within it. We cannot fix every injustice. We cannot withdraw from pain, nor can we deny the weeping and frustration. We cannot always resolve questions that weigh on our hearts. Instead, we must live them. Though we cannot ignore the tensions that surround us, we can continue to choose to receive each twist and turn in the journey as a gift.

It is the journey, the exodus from the old self to the new, that empowers us to explore life, challenge life, make friends with life, poke fun at life, and finally, with courage and good humor, travel the path that moves us closer to becoming the person we were meant to be—to live the life that wants to live in us.

Journaling Gems

Compassion *embodies heartfelt tenderness, thoughtfulness, caring, and responsiveness toward ourselves and others. To act with compassion is to enter into the human condition with loving kindness. Compassion also guides our way from one life experience or plan to the next.*

Journaling Gems

Listening *requires silencing ourselves so as to create an empty space in which we or someone we care about can feel safe exploring, without judgment, ideas, dreams, needs, and fears. Listening paves the way toward a place of wholeness and contentment.*

Journaling Gems

Hospitality *encompasses acts of graciousness and generosity. It begins in the human heart and consists of simple acts of courtesy that provide comfort and consolation. A hospitable heart willingly makes room for change. It also fosters belonging and connection to others.*

Journaling Gems

Hope *represents desire accompanied by expectancy. It defies boundaries and anticipates future good. Hope is larger and more courageous than wishes. Unlike specific expectations that put limitations on life, hope says life can emerge from difficult or chaotic circumstances. Hope refuses to accept misery an option.*

Appendix

Bruce and Sue Kerfoot—A Time for Tenacity

Bruce and Sue Kerfoot took over Gunflint Lodge in the 1960s from Bruce's mother, Justine Kerfoot. The Kerfoot name has been legendary along the Gunflint Trail for decades. The lodge includes a half-mile of Gunflint Lake shoreline with a view into Canada, plus a hundred acres, making it one of the largest resort operations in northern Minnesota. The Gunflint Lodge became the center of a transformation in North Woods recreation, as canoes and backpacks replaced motorized boats and coolers.. The lodge is open year-round and offers everything from fine dining to fabulous walleye fishing, horseback riding, and a zip line canopy tour to take your breath away. Visit the Kerfoots at **gunflint.com.**

Tom Warth Lets His Inspiration Speak

Books for Africa fills once-empty African library shelves in classrooms and in rural schools, as well as the hands of children who have never held a book. Each book is shared among many and read over and over again. They go to children eager to read and eager to explore the world in ways that only books can do. Learn more and visit Tom Warth at booksforafrica.org.

Bruce Ferber—Kiss Your Creativity Hello

Before publishing his debut novel, *Elevating Overman*, Bruce Ferber built a long and successful career as a television comedy writer and producer. A multiple Emmy and Golden Globe nominee, his credits include *Bosom Buddies*; *Growing Pains*; *Sabrina, the Teenage Witch*; *Coach*; and *Home Improvement*, where he served as executive producer. In addition to being recognized by the Television Academy, Ferber's work has received the People's Choice, Kid's Choice, and Environmental Media Awards. His second novel, *Cascade Falls*, was published in March 2015 by Rare Bird Books. He lives in Southern California with his current wife, Lyn; children, Aaron and Sarah; large dog; and assorted musical instruments. Visit him at **bruceferber.net.**

Robin Savage—**Aspire to Accept What Is**

Robin Savage's stand-up performances and speaking engagements entertain without profanity while reflecting her life of motherhood and successful real estate company manager. She is also the face of Ms. Genuity, a crowd-funding site where women and moms, through their collective efforts, can fund, shop, and help shape new products and ventures. Robin lives in Tampa, where she continues to write and perform, and she's always funny. Visit Robin Savage at kwirkybird.com.

Betsy O'Reilly—**the Resourceful Planner**

Betsy O'Reilly, cofounder and CEO of QuadJobs, connects businesses and organizations to local college and graduate students who can make life easier, one job at a time. She lives in Greenwich, Connecticut, with her husband, Ed, and two sons, Magnus and Will. Visit Betsy at quadjobs.com.

Artika Tyner—In Pursuit of Service

Artika Tyner is a passionate educator, author, speaker, and advocate for justice. She serves as a public policy and leadership professor at the University of Saint Thomas in Saint Paul, Minnesota. She also trains graduate students to serve as social engineers who create new inroads to justice and freedom. She received her bachelor's degree from Hamline University. In addition, Artika holds a juris doctor, master's of public policy and leadership, and a doctorate in leadership from the University of Saint Thomas. She is committed to empowering others to lead within their respective spheres of influence. In addition to her teaching, Artika provides leadership development and career coaching for young professionals, as well as educational materials for K–12 students, college and graduate students, faith communities, and nonprofits. Visit Artika at **artikatyner.com**.

Nettie Rosenow—Sometimes a Plan Finds Us

John and Nettie Rosenow live in Waumandee, Wisconsin, where they own and manage Rosenholm Dairy and COWSMO Inc., an affiliated compost business. Nettie also breeds and trains American Quarter Horses. Visit them at cowsmocompost.com or gkrhorses.com.

About the Author:

Mary Farr, a retired pediatric hospital chaplain, teacher, and motivational speaker has devoted more than 30 years to exploring the worlds of hope, healing and humor. Today she has infused these life essentials into her writing, including her wildly funny and gently inspirational book Never Say Neigh. Her capacity to light up audiences with laughter inspires kindness and concern for one another.

Mary has published five books including the critically acclaimed If I Could Mend Your Heart and Peace: Intersections Small Group Series. The Promise in Plan B explores themes of grace and gratitude seasoned with a generous dose of wit.

Mary has been featured in numerous publications, conferences and radio programs and has inspired audiences including women's leadership groups, the Hazelden Foundation, integrative medicine conferences and grief and loss seminars. Through her work, she seeks to shine a light that enables others to discover new meaning and richness within their life journeys.

A graduate of the University of Wisconsin with a Bachelor of Arts degree in English, Mary completed her divinity studies in the Episcopal Diocese of Eau Claire, Wisconsin where she was ordained to the permanent diaconate in 1983. She received a Master of Arts degree from St. Catherine University in her hometown of St. Paul, Minnesota.

CPSIA information can be obtained at www.ICGtesting.com
Printed in the USA
LVOW10s2148161215

466865LV00024B/1021/P

9 780692 513163